Bonhoeffer and King

Bonhoeffer and King: Speaking Truth to Power

J. Deotis Roberts

WESTMINSTER
JOHN KNOX PRESS
LOUISVILLE · KENTUCKY

Scripture quotations from the Revised Standard Version of the Bible are copyright © 1946, 1952, 1971, and 1973 by the Division of Christian Education of the National Council of the Churches of Christ in the U.S.A. and are used by permission.

Excerpt from Elizabeth Raum, *Dietrich Bonhoeffer: Called by God* (New York: Continuum, 2002) is reprinted by permission of The Continuum International Publishing Group. All rights reserved.

Excerpts from Martin Luther King Jr., *Autobiography*, ed. Clayborne Carson (New York: Warner Books, 1998); *Strength to Love* (New York: Harper & Row, 1963); *Stride toward Freedom: The Montgomery Story* (San Francisco: Harper & Row, 1958); *Where Do We Go from Here: Chaos or Community?* (New York: Harper & Row, 1967) are reprinted by arrangement with the Estate of Martin Luther King Jr., c/o Writers House as agent for the proprietor, New York, NY. All rights reserved.

Book design by Sharon Adams
Cover design by Eric Handel, LMNOP

First edition
Published by Westminster John Knox Press
Louisville, Kentucky

This book is printed on acid-free paper that meets the American National Standards Institute Z39.48 standard. ♾

PRINTED IN THE UNITED STATES OF AMERICA

05 06 07 08 09 10 11 12 13 14 — 10 9 8 7 6 5 4 3 2 1

Library of Congress Cataloging-in-Publication Data

Roberts, J. Deotis (James Deotis), 1927–
    Bonhoeffer and King : speaking truth to power / J. Deotis Roberts.—1st ed.
      p. cm.
    Includes bibliographical references.
    ISBN 0-664-22652-3 (alk. paper)
      1. Bonhoeffer, Dietrich, 1906–1945.   2. King, Martin Luther, Jr., 1929–1968.   I. Title.

  BX4827.B57R62 2005
  230'.044'0922—dc22   2004050883

This book is dedicated to my seven grandchildren:

André LaVal Roberts
Jazmin Monét Parker
Elizabeth Tiara Roberts
Arianna Elise Davina Marsh
Ashley Marie Albertha Marsh
David Alonzo Marsh II
Jaxon Wayne Deotis Stewart

May their futures be blessed!

Contents

Contents

Preface

This study is about the Christian witness of Dietrich Bonhoeffer and Martin Luther King Jr. In this volume, I present my understanding of the life, thought, and action of two important Christian theologians of the twentieth century. It is my impression that they "walked into history" and that they left their "footprints on the sands of time." They are treated according to their birth date. The happenings in each country explain the direction of their witness.

It is significant that each was, in his own time and place, a church theologian. It would be demeaning to their firm religious insights and convictions to view them only as social activists. Their quests for social justice had a confessional foundation. It was their profound understanding of the Christian faith that fueled their activism.

Their mission "on earth" reminds us that religious faith can have a positive side. We need this reminder at a time when we are aware that *all religions* may be the sponsors of evil purposes. Their passion for social justice was grounded in the resources of their religious convictions. They reminded us that "humanism" could be Christian. Their lives of witness refute the view that humanism is always completely secular. Theologian Paul Lehmann, a close friend of Bonhoeffer, points to the view held by both of our theologians, that Christian ethics seeks to make life more human. Bonhoeffer and King knew the "human face of God" and advocated the humane use of power.

The study of the early life of any leader is an index to what that person will become in adulthood. There are clues in the formative years of the lives of Bonhoeffer and King that they would make an unusual contribution to humanity during their mature years. Thus, we will look at the contexts of family, personhood, education, and faith-claim in their development. The situation in Nazi Germany is the setting for understanding Bonhoeffer and his mission. We must address the crisis in his life by a careful look at Nazism and the so-called Jewish question. In a similar manner, King's sense of mission is evident in the civil rights movement and his nonviolent effort to bring about the freedom of black people in the United States.

With these perspectives, we will study our subject matter in three parts:

Part 1 intends to get the reader acquainted with each theologian during his early life. We will consider their families, their social status, their education, and their sense of call to be a professor (Bonhoeffer) and minister (King). We will be able to assess their potential by the time they reach adulthood.

Part 2 treats the middle period of their short lives. They were put to death on the eve of what one usually regards as middle life. Each theologian exemplified rapid intellectual and spiritual growth. Both completed a doctorate in theology. Both had pastoral experience, and both embarked upon a ministry or field of service beyond the local parish. Both emphasized love in action, protest against racism and "ethnic cleansing," and both sought to understand collective evils. Bonhoeffer and King had great admiration for Gandhi; in this study, we will examine Gandhi's role as mentor to both theologians in their time and place.

Part 3 is concerned with political theology. We will consider the views of both men on the relation of church to state. Then we will take up the context of decision for Bonhoeffer and King. Separate chapters follow, in which we will assess how each theologian made a decision in his crisis situation. Their decisions cost both of them their lives at thirty-nine years of age. I will attempt to assess the meaning of their lives and witness through death.

The concluding chapter compares some of their essential thoughts and actions—what they believed and how they acted upon these beliefs. We will look at the "common ground" of their witness. Finally, we will observe the continuing influence of Bonhoeffer and King. They pursued the presence of the kingdom of God on earth through their witness. They left open questions. Bonhoeffer asked, "Are we still of any use?" King asked, "Where do we go from here? Chaos or community?" What a challenge! Let us continue their noble pursuit in our time and place.

J. Deotis Roberts
Center of Theological Inquiry
Princeton, New Jersey

Acknowledgments

As an African American Baptist minister and theologian, I have had a long and sustained interest in Dietrich Bonhoeffer and Martin Luther King Jr. I was attracted to them by their theological insights and social justice witness, which I share.

The similarity in the witness of these two church theologians led me to offer advanced seminars comparing their thought and action in context. I taught these seminars at Eastern Baptist Theological Seminary, Lancaster Theological Seminary, Yale Divinity School, and Duke Divinity School. It is my privilege now to express deep appreciation for the dialogue that I have had with faculty members and students, sharing insights and knowledge on this subject matter.

In the 1990s, HarperSanFrancisco published collections of writings by both Bonhoeffer and King. These publications made this vital information readily available for serious study, and they encouraged and enhanced my efforts. These two books are the following: Dietrich Bonhoeffer, *A Testament to Freedom: The Essential Writings of Dietrich Bonhoeffer*, edited by Geffrey B. Kelly and F. Burton Nelson (1995); and Martin Luther King Jr., *A Testament of Hope: The Essential Writings and Speeches of Martin Luther King, Jr.*, edited by James Melvin Washington (1986).

As a member of the International Bonhoeffer Society, I received knowledge and encouragement from colleagues who have spent decades studying Bonhoeffer's life and thought. I will mention only two scholars who provided personal encouragement for this comparative study. Professor Geffrey B. Kelly of LaSalle University in Philadelphia and Professor John Godsey of Wesley Theological Seminary in Washington, DC, have been enthusiastic in their support of my effort to bring these two church theologians together in the comparative study in this volume.

My interest in the life, thought, and action of Martin Luther King Jr. is obvious, since we grew up and made our witness in the same racial context. We belong to the same period of history. We both are sons of the South. I was reared in North Carolina; he grew up in Georgia. We were fellow Baptist ministers in the African American church tradition. Although our areas of service moved along different paths, we were both anchored in the black experience, in family, community, and church as church theologians. His focus was more public, mine more academic.

Even though I had no personal contact with King, I was greatly influenced by his witness. After his death, I became president of the Interdenominational Theological Center in Atlanta. Two of the most outstanding trustees of that institution were "Daddy King" (Martin Luther King Sr.) and Benjamin E. Mays. Coretta King appointed me as a member of the board of directors of the King Center. This encounter with the King family has been an additional inspiration for this study.

I am grateful for the two men who assisted me in the research for this manuscript. For three years, during my term as Research Professor of Theology at Duke Divinity School, the Reverend Johnny B. Hill served as my research assistant. He is now pursuing a PhD at Garrett Theological Seminary. Paul Ogden Ford, a longtime family friend who now is engaged in advanced studies at the Free University in Berlin, has been a resourceful assistant. While in Berlin for a Bonhoeffer conference, Ford was a guide and interpreter for my wife and me. He has done research in the Bonhoeffer archives in Berlin. He was especially helpful during a preaching event I had at the Dietrich Bonhoeffer Kirchengemeinde in Berlin. He was the official interpreter for my sermon and subsequent conversation with Pastor Hartmut Walsdorff.

I also wish to acknowledge those who participated in the final preparation of this volume. Donald McKim, an editor at Westminster John Knox Press, invited me to submit a proposal for this volume in its conception phase. He soon offered to publish the work and has followed the process with helpful suggestions. A warm word of thanks is extended to Julie Tonini, whose editorial skills have greatly improved the manner in which the message in this book has been presented. Melody Mazuk, library director at Eastern Baptist Theological Seminary, has encouraged this process. She also made contact with Jeron Frame, who has skillfully prepared this manuscript for publication. I acknowledge all these persons with a vote of thanks.

In the fall of 2003, I was invited to become a member of the Center of Theological Inquiry in Princeton, New Jersey. The dialogue with several theologians who are residents at the CTI, members of the Princeton Theological Seminary faculty, as well as visitors to the CTI, have greatly enhanced my efforts. This period of quiet reflection, together with library resources at the seminary and university, came at the best time to enrich my study. I wish to express my thanks to Kathi Morley, program director, and the Reverend Wallace Alston, executive director, together with all members of the CTI staff for their hospitality and assistance. A theological student at Princeton Theological Seminary, Danté Quick, was a dutiful and indispensable assistant. I give him a profound vote of thanks.

Finally, I must acknowledge the love and nurture of my family. I must remember my son, Deotis, who perished in a tragic automobile accident at age 19, and the passing away of a granddaughter, Jewell, in her infancy. My wife, Elizabeth, has supported me with deep affection and understanding for more than fifty years. My three daughters, Charmaine, Carlita, and Kristina, have always been near and dear. My seven grandchildren are a great inspiration. This volume is dedicated to their futures.

To all who have encouraged this study and dialogued with me, I am deeply grateful. However, I take full responsibility for the outcome of what I have presented here. If others are inspired to pursue this subject matter, I will be both honored and rewarded.

Part I
Life Stories

1

Introduction:
Person, Time, and Place

AUTOBIOGRAPHICAL REFLECTIONS

We begin this introduction with an attempt to get acquainted with the persons whose life and witness to God and humanity are being explored. The topic of an essay by Lerone Bennett is suggestive. Bennett writes concerning what he describes as "When the man and the hour are met."[1] As we explore the life and witness of both Martin Luther King Jr. and Dietrich Bonhoeffer, we encounter the meeting of person, time, and place.

Before we begin, some autobiographical reflections may be useful. I am an African American, a theologian, and an ordained Baptist minister. I was born in the South (North Carolina) in 1927. I was ordained in 1946. I have pastored churches in North Carolina, Connecticut, and Scotland. As professor, I have taught in seminaries and universities across this nation. I have also been a seminary dean and president. I have, therefore, shared much by the way of time, space, and experience with our two subjects.

I am a son of the South. I belong to King's generation. Like him, I am a minister-theologian. In my own way, I have shared his struggle for the liberation of black people from the evils of racial discrimination.

Many experiences that shaped King's outlook have helped to frame my own life and ministry. While my ministry has been primarily academic, his ministry was anchored in the church. He was drawn from that setting into the civil rights movement. Though my anchor has been in the academy, my heart has been in the church. One colleague captured well my outlook. He observed, "Roberts is a theologian with a pastor's heart." My location in the academy has kept me close to future pastors as well as to active church leaders. Much of my writing has focused upon ministry as well.

I was studying for my PhD at the University of Edinburgh when I heard of the leadership of King in the civil rights movement. During this same period, I was interim pastor of the Radnor Park Congregational Church in Glasgow, Scotland. At the conclusion of my study, I was called for the pastorate of that congregation. However, directly related to the awareness of the powerful witness of King, I readily decided to return to the United States to continue my ministry. I was on leave from Shaw University in Raleigh, North Carolina, to complete my graduate study. There I had been professor and college minister.

I was awarded the PhD by the University of Edinburgh in 1957. One year later, I was appointed to a professorship as theologian at Howard University's School of Religion (now Divinity School). My work at Howard was very demanding and involved a lot of interdisciplinary teaching.[2]

The involvement of Howard University in the civil rights movement was, at this time, focused upon constitutional law. Howard University lawyers such as Thurgood Marshall and Spottswood Robinson were leading attorneys in the Supreme Court's 1954 *Brown v. Board of Education* decision. After a summer seminar on theology and law at Duke Divinity School, led by Professor Waldo Beach, I joined Dean Spottswood Robinson of the law school in leading a seminar on religion and law at Howard. The course brought together students and faculty in both disciplines around common concerns.

Books and articles that I released during this period demonstrate my interest in the civil rights movement and King's leadership. It was my privilege to hear King lecture and preach on several occasions. I did not personally meet him. My study abroad, my heavy academic load at Howard, and the need to re-enter the academy and church after my absence explain somewhat this lack of contact with King. It was certainly not the absence of interest in his mission. Dialogue with him would have been very rewarding, and I am certain my life and this study would have been enriched and strengthened by such a personal encounter. My Atlanta period, though very important, was no substitute for this omission.

This account of the inspiration that I received from the witness of King's ministry is important. It explains some of the passion given to what follows. So much of King's development is similar to mine that the insights of his thought and life will be reflected throughout my discussion. The emphasis on reconciliation in my program of black theology echoes the message of "love" in King's thought. However, the theme of "liberation" plugs into the "black power" motif of black theology.[3]

As I turn to Bonhoeffer, I cannot claim the same close identification with his life and thought. Nevertheless, the study of his life and thought has made a similar impact upon my thinking. Bonhoeffer, like King, was a church theologian and activist for social justice.

While engaged in advanced study in the United States, I was not given an adequate introduction to Bonhoeffer. He was studied along with other German thinkers; however, he was overshadowed by Karl Barth, Rudolf Bultmann, and others. By the middle of the 1960s, however, Bonhoeffer was given attention in the United States among the death-of-God theologians. This view of Bonhoeffer did not impress me or other black liberation theologians.

While engaged in PhD studies at the University of Edinburgh in the mid-1950s, I was privileged to hear the lectures of Professor John Baillie, who became one of my advisors. Baillie had seen firsthand the potential of Dietrich Bonhoeffer as a theologian. Baillie had taught Bonhoeffer at Union Theological Seminary in New York City.[4] He insisted that his students at Edinburgh treat Bonhoeffer's thought seriously. He claimed that if Bonhoeffer had survived the Second World War, he would have been equal in status to Barth as a theologian. This was quite a statement at Edinburgh, where Professor Thomas Torrance was a major English-speaking advocate of the thought of Barth.

This high estimate of Bonhoeffer as theologian lingered in my mind. Theologians in England and the United States did not seem to me to take Bonhoeffer seriously. They read some of his works mainly for devotional purposes, or they read his *Letters* as representative of a robust humanism. Nevertheless, they seemed to have missed his profound message of liberation for those who are oppressed. When I joined the International Bonhoeffer Society, I wondered why suffering people the world over were moved by Bonhoeffer's thought and life. When I asked one outstanding Bonhoeffer scholar why Bonhoeffer was receiving global attention, he replied, "This is so because Bonhoeffer identified with those who suffer."[5]

In addition to this encouraging introduction, I began a careful study of Bonhoeffer's life and thought as I developed my own program of black theology. I desired to know more about his life and activities from all of his writings. In several advanced seminars over the years at a number of seminaries and universities, I entered into dialogue with students who shared my desire to learn from Bonhoeffer about social justice issues. The result is this effort to commit to the printed page his powerful witness to the mission of the Christian church and the mandates of the gospel for the liberation of oppressed peoples.

It was during my involvement with the black church struggle for freedom that my interest in Bonhoeffer and King reached a high level of attention. It became meaningful to bring them together in a comparative study. My students were attracted to a serious study of these theologians as well.

When I began reflecting upon the problem of collective evil that is inherent in racism, I realized the importance of the witness of these two church theologians. I realized the power and purpose of their message to humankind. It became obvious to me that they in their contexts *spoke truth to power*. They

left for us superb examples of public theologies for the liberation and reconciliation of peoples around the globe.

THE PROBLEM

This study will explore the views of Bonhoeffer and King concerning the relation of state and church. We will consider the nature and function of state and
church and how these two institutions relate to each other in the thought and
action of Bonhoeffer and King. In order to explore this subject matter, we must
raise questions regarding the nature and use or abuse of political power.
"Speaking truth to power" presents a challenge for thought and action in both
spheres of human life. Bonhoeffer and King make it clear that Christians are
summoned to think and act in these spheres of our experience.

Words are highly suggestive of the concerns Bonhoeffer and King had as
they faced a form of collective evil in the political order. Their stance, as they
stood securely in the church as theologians, was "prophetic" as they confronted abuses of political power in the social order. In both contexts, forms
of evil (i.e., racism and anti-Semitism) were manifest. In both cases, church
and state were implicated in the existence of a form of oppression of a sizeable
segment of human beings. Bonhoeffer and King, in their time and place, summoned the courage, anchored in their Christian faith, to confront these evils
with an ultimate devotion to truth and freedom.

Through an examination of the writings and testimonies of Bonhoeffer and
King, we note careful reflection on the meanings of "truth" and "power."
While we may assume a simple and clear understanding of the meaning of both
terms, we will observe in the course of our study that, when faced with crisis,
these theologians were intellectually and spiritually challenged. Yet they finally
offered up their lives for the sake of what they believed to be true. Augustine
is reported to have observed that we know what "love" is until we are asked to
define it. The same could be said about "truth."

"Power" also has a troubling meaning. The apostle Paul made a statement
that has a dubious meaning in the history of human politics: "There is no power
but of God: the powers that be are ordained of God" (Rom. 13:1 KJV). We can
assume that the reference is to Rome. If this is the case, we need also to read
Revelation 13. I here repeat an insight from Allen Boesak speaking of the
apartheid era in South Africa. Both Bonhoeffer and King were gravely concerned about the meaning of "power" and its use and abuse in church and political arenas.

I raise these issues regarding the meaning of my theme to alert the reader
to what is to come. Yet I use this language to prepare the reader for the pow-

erful message regarding the two theologians and their witness in what Jack Forstman has appropriately described as "dark times."[6]

The problem of evil has been described as an enigma within a mystery. I will not attempt to discuss this problem in depth here; I have explored it in other contexts.[7] Here we raise the issue as it relates to our subject matter. Bonhoeffer and King were concerned about collective or systemic evil as expressed in their national life. Nazism and segregation were their targets, and these evils had infested both church and state. In their view, the gospel of Jesus Christ is opposed to evil, wherever it is found. Standing as they did within the church, they engaged in "internal" and "external" prophecy. Bonhoeffer attacked the so-called German Christians, who embraced Nazism, while King confronted segregationists who had turned the church into a racist institution. They challenged Christians to be true to the Lord of the church and unite against the evils in the social order. Only the "true" church, in their judgment, could be effective in opposing collective evils in the social order. They sought an understanding of the gospel that would lead to radical social transformation. A "soul-and-savior gospel," focused upon the individual only, is not adequate to deal with evil, which has spread like a cancer in the body politic. There is a need for salvation that transforms the inner life. Nevertheless, there needs to be more than this. Bonhoeffer and King sponsored a version of Christianity that sought to transform the national life of Germany and the United States.

DISCOURSE ON METHODS

I have made reference to more than one method to be used in my exposition in this volume. The subject matter of this book is so rich and diverse that I concluded that to do justice to this task, I should opt for several approaches to the interpretation of the material at hand.

First, I am impressed with the theological method introduced by James W. McClendon Jr., which he calls "biography as theology."[8] The first part of this book will employ this method, as I give attention to the life story of each theologian in his particular location and time. We will then examine some essential aspects of their early development in order to target their emergence as adults, as scholars, and as minister-theologians and activists.

Second, once we have viewed Bonhoeffer and King on the way to adulthood and their taking hold of their vocation as minister-theologians, we will engage some of the essentials of their theological thought. Once we have viewed their thought, with an eye toward the essentials of their corpus, we will examine a concise dialogue on their theology and ethics.[9] This will allow us to compare and contrast their views on some concrete events and issues that they both confront with thought and action. One example is racism; another is political oppression. The latter will be the focus of part 3 of this study and will not be treated in depth in part 2. The method of theological analysis will serve our purpose in this section.

Finally, we will deal with the mature commitments of each theologian to the liberation of the oppressed. Their solidarity with those who suffer due to a collective evil is where their witness converges. Thus, we will be dealing with praxis in this section. The insights of liberation theologies will be useful in this section and will be used to explicate their life of witness against collective evil. Contextualization will be used also.

We will draw insights from three or more theological methods that have been used in theological discourse in recent years. We will, of course, be using some methods that ethicists have defined. These will be referenced and used as appropriate. We are treating two important and seminal thinkers and leaders of the twentieth century. Therefore, these several methods of discourse will be useful as we move forward.

CONCLUSION

In this chapter, I have raised a few issues to introduce both the author and the subject under discussion. First, it has been my purpose to indicate how I became interested in a serious account of the life, thought, and witness of Bonhoeffer and King. I have a personal affinity with these church theologians with a focus on social justice. The autobiographical reasons fueled my intense interest in this study. Second, I have presented a theme that brings a forceful announcement of what is to be expected in this study. I delimit necessarily the range of my interest. My focus is on church-state concerns, yet my theme will allow us to get to the essentials of the life, thought, and witness of Bonhoeffer and King. "Speaking truth to power" seems to state symbolically, if not literally, my intention. A subtopic is my conception of collective evil inherent in sinful social and political structures. My overall purpose is to view the gospel through the lenses of our theologians as a means to redeem and transform social and national life. In the next chapter we will get better acquainted with our theologians.

2

Biography as Theology

During many years of the study of philosophical and religious thinkers, it became obvious that there is a relationship between the historic and social situation of a thinker and her or his thought. Knowledge of milieu is key to the character of life, thought, and action. Humans are free beings. However, our freedom for thought and action is within certain limits. We are impacted by the situation in which we live. Not only is our cultural context an index to self-understanding, but the more intimate relations in family life have their imprint upon our lives—who we are and who we become. With these observations in view, we will have a closer look at Bonhoeffer and King. First, we will examine the social contexts of their decisions.

THE GERMAN SITUATION

Bonhoeffer came to his own as a church theologian and ethicist in Germany under the rule of Adolf Hitler. In order to understand Bonhoeffer's powerful witness, one needs to survey briefly the German situation in the early twentieth century.[1]

At the end of the First World War, there was much suffering on the part of the German people. Harsh terms were imposed by the countries that won the war. The Versailles Treaty reclaimed much German land, limited Germany's army to one hundred thousand men, deprived Germany of colonies, and prevented Germany from uniting with Austria. In addition, Germany was forced to accept the "war guilt clause." This meant the acceptance of responsibility for the war and the payment of reparations to other nations.

As a result of these measures, Germans willingly embraced nationalism. They were willing to defend their country at all costs. Many Germans were looking for scapegoats to blame for their troubles. It only required a "leader" to inflame these deeply felt emotions. It was not too difficult for Hitler, an evil messiah-like figure, to fuel this anger. He seized upon a long tradition of anti-Semitism and blamed the Jews for Germany's woes. He used the false notion of racial purity to rally non-Jewish Germans against Jewish friends and neighbors.

In a similar manner, we will need to look at the racial situation in the middle of the twentieth century to appreciate the witness of Martin Luther King Jr. Some knowledge of black slavery is important to putting the issues of the civil rights movement in context. The evil of slavery has cast a shadow over the entire history of race relations in U.S. society. The Holocaust and slavery symbolize the tragic events resulting from anti-Semitism in Germany and racism in the United States. Both evils have led to genocide in their time and place.

I was asked by a group of liberal Jewish leaders to provide a study of anti-Semitism fostered by scholars of biblical studies in American seminaries. These leaders had a special interest in those seminaries with a sizeable number of black students. The purpose of the study was to lead to a better understanding between Jews and blacks through dialogue between Jewish and black religious leaders. When I suggested that a comparison be made between the Holocaust and slavery as these evils had impacted each people, I was surprised to hear that this type of study would be unfair to Jews. Jewish leaders often have said that the Holocaust should be remembered to make sure that it will never happen again. To me, it seemed logical to view slavery in the same light. Both events are intergenerational. Such a comparative study would be useful for blacks as well as Jews. Blacks need to know more about the curse of anti-Semitism, while Jews need to know how blacks live in the shadow of slavery. An in-depth study of the life, thought, and witness of Bonhoeffer and King could be useful in viewing the important encounter between Jews and blacks.

In my conversation with liberal Jews, I became aware that some of my Jewish friends considered King to be a great leader. They had participated in civil rights marches and heard his "I have a dream" speech in Washington, DC. However, they were not aware that King's "dream" became a "nightmare" before his death. Much of King's disappointment with race relations came to him in the North as well as the South. In the language of Vincent Harding, King became "an inconvenient hero."[2]

Bonhoeffer's decision to study theology came as a shock to his entire family, although his mother may have been an exception. Bonhoeffer was fourteen when he and his twin sister, Sabine, studied for confirmation. They took classes with Pastor Priebe at the Grunewald Church. The German Evangelical churches held separate classes for girls and boys. Instruction was given in church history, church doctrine, and the Bible. Dietrich and Sabine went together to church and sometimes discussed the sermons. Dietrich had begun to devote considerable time to Bible study. He showed real concern for spiritual matters. His closest friends began asking him religious questions.

Soon after confirmation at age fourteen, Bonhoeffer announced to his family that he intended to become a theologian. His brothers and sisters did not take him seriously. This led him to be more serious about his decision. Karl-Friedrich was studying natural science, and Klaus was studying law. They tried to convince Dietrich that the church was not worthy of his time and attention. His father also attempted to suggest that his gifts were too outstanding to be given to the church. Dietrich was determined to cling to his decision. His response was, "In that case, I shall reform it!" He chose to take Hebrew as his optional subject at school and began attending church with his mother. Thus, the members of his family realized that his decision was firm.

Eberhard Bethge, who became Dietrich's best friend and biographer, observes several factors that may have led to this decision. His brother Walter's death in the First World War and his mother's grief renewed his own belief in eternal life. He desired to share this hope with others. He felt a gulf between himself and his brothers, who excelled in the study of the natural sciences. Unlike them, he was attracted to spiritual matters. He sensed a loneliness for God. His study of theology did not involve church attendance or Bible reading; it was more of a philosophical approach to ultimate reality.

He explored knowledge among the ancient Greek philosophers, German theologians such as Schleiermacher, and his own great-grandfather, Karl August von Hase. Once his career decision had been made, his friends noted a "radiance" in his temperament. He was soon at the University of Tübingen, according to a family tradition. His brothers, Karl-Friedrich and Klaus, and his sister Christine were studying there. Dietrich joined them as a theologian in the making.

BONHOEFFER'S FAMILY LIFE

In order to understand Bonhoeffer's life, it is important to look at his family heritage. Dietrich Bonhoeffer came from a rich cultural background. The Bonhoeffers were immigrants from Holland (van den Boenhoff from Nimwegen). In the sixteenth century, they had been mainly goldsmiths. From the seventeenth century, the family had in its ranks clergy, doctors, councilors, and mayors.[3]

Dietrich's paternal grandfather was Friedrich von Bonhoeffer (1828–1907). Friedrich was president of the provincial court in Ulm. Dietrich's paternal grandmother was Julie Bonhoeffer (1842–1936). Her life overlapped with Dietrich's youth. In old age, Julie opposed the boycott of Jewish businesses, which began on April 1, 1933. Dietrich was very close to his grandmother and embraced much of her moral courage against social injustice.

On Dietrich's mother's side, there were outstanding religious leaders. His grandfather, Karl Alfred von Hase (1842–1914), became a divisional chaplain in Hanover. He later became a senior army chaplain in Königsberg. He married Clara, née Countess von Kalckreuth (1851–1903). Their daughter, Paula von Hase, was Dietrich's mother. In 1889, Karl Alfred von Hase was nominated court preacher in Potsdam by Wilhelm II. Two years later he resigned. From 1894 he was consistory councilor and professor of practical theology in Breslau. Dietrich's great-grandfather Karl August von Hase (1800–1890) had been professor of church history and the history of dogma at Jena. He was influenced by Schleiermacher, "the one who conquered theological rationalism," according to his estimation. When Dietrich was a student, he valued his great-grandfather's textbook on the history of dogma as a help toward passing examinations.

Dietrich's mother insisted on taking the teacher's examination for her role as mother. Later she used her teacher's certification in middle and high school education to teach her own children in their early years. The children were not only homeschooled in the early years; they received much of their religious instruction from their mother. For occasions such as baptisms, they invited clergy in the family, including Dietrich's grandfather von Hase and his mother's brother, Klaus von Hase.

In 1912, Karl Bonhoeffer was called to the Friedrich Wilhelm University in Berlin. As director of the *Charité*, the University Nerve Clinic, he took the leading chair of psychiatry and neurology in Germany. In outlook he was empirical in his judgments; he would not go beyond what he had experienced.

Dietrich was reared in a family of eight children. His sister Sabine was his twin. Among the boys he was the youngest. There were two sisters between Dietrich and his older three brothers. He was especially close to Sabine and Susanne, the youngest child. This birth order may have had some importance for Dietrich, which we will explore later. The family was extended in the sense that the kinship among relatives was cordial and close. It was certainly intergenerational. I have already noted the affectionate ties between Dietrich and his grandmother.

Karl Bonhoeffer was proud of his children. He once observed that "there were not too many of them." As busy as he was as both a teaching and practicing psychiatrist, he spent quality time with his children. He provided a holiday venue for the family where he could play with them. After supper on Sundays, he would read stories to his children. He was the authority figure in the family, insofar as the children were concerned. He appears to have been a person of remarkable moral character, an excellent adult role model for his children as husband and father. Though not a confessing Christian, he exemplified admirable humanistic values.

The family spirit was wholesome for the Bonhoeffer children. Every Sunday evening there was a musical event in the home. The family would gather in the salon, where the three older boys would begin by playing a trio: Klaus played the piano, Karl-Friedrich played the cello, and Walter played the violin. Maria Horn, governess to the Bonhoeffer children, accompanied Paula, the mother, while she sang. All the children performed something. The sisters sang duets, and Dietrich played the piano. Dietrich surpassed his older brother on the piano. His parents even entertained the idea that he might become a professional musician. Although his career took another turn, his musical abilities served him well in his practical ministry to come.

In 1914, the First World War began. This impacted the Bonhoeffer family directly when the second-oldest son, Walter, was wounded in battle and died on April 28, 1918. Sabine and Dietrich heard much talk about death among their classmates who had lost family members in the war. The children "tried to get nearer to eternity" in their thoughts and prayers. Walter's death brought great pain to their mother, who was bedfast for a period of time.

It is important to mention the friendship that existed between the Bonhoeffers and their neighbors during Dietrich's formative years. In 1916, the family moved to the Grunewald area of Berlin, to 14 Wangenheimstrasse, near Halensee Station. Many noted scholars lived nearby. Fritz Mauthner, a noted philosopher, was there. Max Planck, Nobel Prize winner in physics (1918), was a neighbor. Historian Hans Delbrück, theologians Adolf von Harnack and Ernst Troeltsch, and others were neighbors and belonged to a discussion group with Karl Bonhoeffer. The sons and daughters of families in this community got to know each other, and later there were marriages between them. Many of these youths reunited as adults in the struggle against Hitler.

KING'S FAMILY LIFE

The roots of King's family life are deep in the South. King's family beginnings were in slavery. Little has been written concerning his great-grandfather. We do know some details concerning the lives of his grandfather and grandmothers through the autobiographical accounts of King's father, affectionately known as "Daddy King."[4]

Daddy King spent his early life in Stockbridge, about eighteen miles outside Atlanta. He was a sharecropper's son. Sharecropping was the only option available for many blacks immediately after slavery. Blacks, most of whom lived in abject poverty, did much of the hard work on the farm, while whites reaped the economic benefits. The plantation owner would dole out a small amount from the sale of farm products to each sharecropper. Daddy King once observed that his father was being cheated by his boss. When Daddy King, as a boy, spoke out against this injustice, he was threatened by the plantation owner. King's father cautioned his son to keep quiet. He was almost totally dependent upon his boss for economic security. However, Daddy King made up his mind to leave the farm.

Daddy King's mother was a devout woman. She was also courageous and physically strong. She once took on a white man who abused her son. Unfortunately, Daddy King's father turned to excessive drinking to soothe his pain. He would physically abuse his wife. When Daddy King was in his teens, he was robust and strong. After being forced to take on his father in defense of his mother, he knew it was best to leave home.[5]

As a teenager, King joined a sister in Atlanta. He took a job on a train, feeding the coal engine. When his mother discovered what he was doing, she had him removed from this job due to his youth. But King had made up his mind to stay in Atlanta, so he made other arrangements. At eighteen, he started out to get a high school education. This was difficult, since he had to begin at the beginning and was much older than his classmates. Nevertheless, with his mind made up, he continued his study until he graduated from Morehouse College.

King married Alberta Williams, daughter of A. D. Williams, pastor of Ebenezer Baptist Church in Atlanta, on November 25, 1926. King was at that time pastor of a small congregation. He later became an assistant to Williams, and upon Williams's death, became his successor. Martin Jr. was born on January 18, 1929. The birth of a sister and a brother followed. Daddy King, his wife, and their three children lived at 193 Boulevard in Atlanta. Martin Jr.'s grandmother, Jennie Celeste Williams, lived in the same house. Martin Jr. was nurtured in an intergenerational, extended family. His grandmother was near and dear to him.

Martin Jr. described his mother as a caring and approachable person. She also was a devout Christian. While King's father was outspoken, she was soft-spoken and easygoing. She had grown up in comparative comfort, protected from the worst blights of discrimination. An only child, she had received a good education. However, she never accepted in a passive manner the system of segregation around her. She instilled a sense of self-respect in all of her children.

Martin Jr. described his father as a genuine Christian in character. He was deeply committed to moral principles. Martin Sr. was known for his frankness, but he always expressed outstanding and sincere motives and actions. He sought to tell the truth and speak his mind.[6]

Daddy King had a strong interest in civil rights. At one time he was president of the NAACP in Atlanta. He refused to ride city buses, and fought for equal pay for black teachers, the elimination of Jim Crow elevators, and the right to vote for black citizens. He was much respected in the black community and won the grudging respect of some whites.[7]

When I moved to Macon in 1952, I visited Atlanta and sought a conversation with Daddy King. The meeting with King's father in his home with his wife and daughter was very cordial. However, Martin Jr. was not home; he was in Boston at the time. This was my first encounter with Daddy King and was a memorable event.

Many years later, I became president of the Interdenominational Theological Center in Atlanta. I was surprised to find that Daddy King was a member of that institution's board of trustees. As a fellow Baptist, he along with President Emeritus Benjamin E. Mays became a strong supporter of my new role. More than that, they were my personal mentors. One of the highlights of my time in Atlanta was the fellowship I experienced with them both. I can personally affirm the testimony of Martin Jr. concerning his father. In many contexts, I witnessed a person who was frank, forceful, and trustworthy in support of what he believed to be right. Daddy King seemed to have a temperament different from his son. Nevertheless, he often made it clear that he believed in the ethic of nonviolence advocated by his son.

Martin Jr. had a comfortable childhood. His father was a good provider for his family. The church was his second home. His parents, grandmother, and fellow siblings were constantly involved in church activities. He joined the church at five years of age, while attending Sunday school. This act was not done out of thoughtful conviction; he joined because his sister had joined before him. His encounter with Scripture at this time was literal. His teachers of the Bible were unlettered and fundamentalist in belief. However, this was not to last, given his inquisitive mind. At age thirteen, he shocked his Sunday school class by denying the bodily resurrection of Jesus.

Martin Jr.'s call to ministry is of special interest. At age fifteen, King entered Morehouse College. King's maternal grandfather and his father had studied there. It was at Morehouse that he began a thoughtful quest to overcome racial injustice. He studied under professors who were free to think and express their opinions.

Upon entering college, King found himself interested in political matters and social ills. He read Henry David Thoreau's essay "On Civil Disobedience" many times. Upon considering Thoreau's message, he became convinced that noncooperation with evil is as much a moral obligation as is cooperation with good. Following the example of his parents, King felt the urge to serve society. Law and medicine came to mind as professions that he might enter to fulfill his desire to help others. In the meantime, his childhood exposure to religion had laid a claim upon him. However, the brand of religion he had been exposed to was fundamentalism. He was in revolt against the extreme emotionalism he had encountered and the unlettered ministers and teachers who had sponsored it. He became extremely skeptical about the relation of science to religion. He decided to major in sociology. This was a fortunate decision, which pointed to his future.

A course in biblical studies under George Kelsey, professor of philosophy of religion, calmed his doubts, and the presence of Benjamin Mays as president of the college was a real help. Both Kelsey and Mays were minister-scholars. They represented the type of minister King aspired to be. King had been interested in ministry from his high school days, but doubts had blocked the urge. Now the urge appeared as an inescapable drive. He was aware of the powerful influence of his father. Though his father had never pressured him to enter the ministry, he knew his father would be pleased. At the age of nineteen, as King finished college, he accepted the ministry as his calling. He described his call to ministry thus: "My call to the ministry was not a miraculous or supernatural something. On the contrary, it was an inner urge calling me to serve humanity."[8]

THE FAMILY HERITAGES OF BONHOEFFER AND KING COMPARED

In this discussion I have assumed that the years of growing up, from birth to adulthood, are very important for a leader's life commitment and contribution to humankind through service. This is especially true for persons like Bonhoeffer and King, who had a praxis orientation to life.

In demonstrating this point, I have thus far explored the developmental phase of their early lives. The psychosocial growth of each theologian-activist indicates that both embarked upon a journey or pilgrimage of service to humankind. This for each was anchored in an understanding of faith. For Bonhoeffer and King there was a sense of response, both personal and social, to a special summons, an urge to participate in a project that would bring about social changes for the betterment of the human condition.

Neither of these two religious leaders claimed a sudden, certain, emotional "call" to be a minister. However, the urge to be such was internal, persistent, and undeniable. Both expressed relief and joy at their respective moments of decision. Their time of witness would be brief but decisive. As we observe their period of study, their intellectual and spiritual growth, and their early stage of ministry, we can note a confirmation of the urge to minister in their teen years.

Bonhoeffer, as we have seen, had a respectable if not a regal ancestry. His father had a solid social and economic position in the academy and community. He was able to house, feed, and educate a large family in troubled times.

King, in his social context, was equally blessed. He was nurtured and affirmed in a loving family and a warm church fellowship. His father was a responsible family man and a good provider. Unlike many of his contemporaries among blacks, King had the solid economic support of his father during his time of growing up. By comparison, he had a life of privilege in his social environment, especially among members of his race in a segregated society.

Despite their social advantages, both theologians felt called to serve those who suffer most in their social environment. Our study will explore why they saw their mission as one to liberate the oppressed. What led them to see needs and adverse conditions from "below" rather than from a position of privilege? Answers to this type of question will deepen our appreciation of the depths of their obedience to the will of God as they understood it.

3

Academic and Spiritual Growth

The early years of adulthood are important in assessing the future possibilities of a leader. This is especially true in the case of Bonhoeffer and King. They both lived a short life. One usually looks at the forties as the best years in the life of a leader; they lost their lives at thirty-nine. Thus, a look at the formative years of their early adulthood is crucial for understanding their powerful witness to social justice in their respective times and places.

BONHOEFFER'S FORMATIVE YEARS

In the middle of his teen years (adolescence), Dietrich Bonhoeffer surprised his family by announcing that he intended to be a theologian. Thus began a life journey whose course he could not have fully understood at the time. We will briefly chart this course as he prepared for his life's work.[1]

As a theological student at Tübingen, Dietrich studied some of Martin Luther's thought under Adolf Schlatter. He knew enough Hebrew to study the Psalms and the prophets. He was gripped by the passion of the prophets for social justice. He attended lectures by Heitmüller on Romans, where he read Karl Barth's *Epistle to the Romans*. He also studied with Karl Heim. He did not share Heim's interest in science; nevertheless, it was through Heim that he was introduced to Schleiermacher. Karl Müller's course in medieval church history aroused his interest in Rome. While in this class, Dietrich planned a visit to Rome, which he and his brother Klaus undertook in the spring of 1924.

Dietrich fell under the spell of Catholic Rome. He met a priest in Bologna who became his guide during Holy Week in Rome. Dietrich was moved by the richness of the liturgy as well as the devotion of the people. The deeply spiritual nature of the confession was upon his mind for a lifetime.

Dietrich was at a mass in St. Peter's on Palm Sunday. There he encountered the universality of the Catholic Church. He compared it in his mind with the parochialism of his German Protestantism. However, his intellectual criticism of Catholicism remained. He saw a great difference between the act of confession and the dogma of confession.

After a brief trip to North Africa with Klaus, Dietrich returned to Berlin for serious study at Berlin University from 1924 to 1927. There Dietrich engaged in intense theological study. He was now only nineteen. At the university, Dietrich encountered church historian Adolf von Harnack and Luther scholar Karl Holl. Reinhold Seeberg became his dissertation advisor. It was under Seeberg's direction that Dietrich produced his initial doctoral document, "The Communion of Saints." In this work, Bonhoeffer used sociology and social philosophy to aid in his theological interpretation of the church. This work was in keeping with the liberal theological tradition at Berlin. One only needs to recall the influence of Schleiermacher, Hegel, and Troeltsch to confirm this. Bonhoeffer asserted that the transcendence of God is moral and social. It is not an abstract idea. God is as close as the nearby neighbor in need.

This dissertation was completed in 1927 when Bonhoeffer was only 21. In this work, he declared that the church is "Christ existing as community." For him, the church was neither an ideal society without need of reform, nor a gathering of the gifted elite. It was as much a communion of sinners as it was a communion of saints for whom serving one another should be a delight.

Bonhoeffer was off to Barcelona in 1928, in the midst of the worldwide Great Depression, to accept an appointment as assistant pastor. He was to minister to the needs of the German business community. This assignment provided him with the practical experience he needed for ordination. Parish life in Barcelona gave Bonhoeffer his first serious encounter with poverty. He plunged into a ministry to help the unemployed. He even asked his family for financial assistance. This experience enhanced the power of his preaching.

When Bonhoeffer returned to Berlin, he wrote a second doctoral dissertation, which was required for an appointment to the university faculty. *Act and Being* was published as a book in 1931. Here Bonhoeffer worked on a theory of knowledge that would help him understand revelation. This seems to have been an indication of his personal struggle to clarify a vocational place to stand—in the academy or in the church. Later in this study we will look more closely at this phase of his life.

Bonhoeffer then went to New York City. He had accepted a Sloane Fellowship to study at Union Theological Seminary for the academic year 1930–1931. At Union, Dietrich encountered a theological climate of liberal humanism. He was pleased to meet such thinkers as Reinhold Niebuhr and John Baillie (a guest professor from Scotland).

Persons Bonhoeffer met and befriended at Union aroused his interest in the message of the Sermon on the Mount. But his two most important relationships were with two people who aroused his concern for the critical issues of racism and peace.

Frank Fisher, an African American from Alabama, introduced Bonhoeffer to the Harlem community and especially to the Abyssinian Baptist Church. Attending this church, listening to the sermons of Adam Clayton Powell Sr., and teaching Sunday school made Bonhoeffer sensitive to the depths of the racial divide in the United States. This awareness of the pain of racism upon victims as well as the plight of slum dwellers in their poverty would be with him for the rest of his life.

Another friend, French pacifist Jean Lasserre, transformed Bonhoeffer's life. In spite of the French-German conflict, these two friends shared a desire for world peace. Under Jean's influence, Bonhoeffer became devoted to non-violent resistance to evil. Bonhoeffer took this passion for peace into his ecumenical work.

Bonhoeffer was a different person when he returned from America. He was interested in international relations as well as the downtrodden in the slums of Berlin. At twenty-five he began to live life fully committed to the teachings of Christ. He attended church services regularly, meditated daily on Bible passages, and included prayer and confession as a daily part of his life. He frequently cited the Sermon on the Mount as a basis for Christian action. His friends and associates noticed his new outlook. Bonhoeffer appeared happy with his commitment to the life of the church.

Until this time his desire had been to be a theologian in a scholarly manner. But now, as Bonhoeffer observed, "the theologian became a Christian." Henceforth he was to be one of the most outstanding church theologians of the twentieth century.

MARTIN LUTHER KING JR.: YEARS OF PREPARATION

Martin Luther King Jr. had an unusual experience of ministerial preparation. He grew up in the church. His father was a preacher, and so were his grandfather and great-grandfather. But in spite of this churchly background, entering the ministry was a personal struggle, as we shall see.[2]

With this anchor in the church, King's progress in his calling was given strong moral and financial support. Advancement in this field was extremely difficult for those who had no support in the home and little in the church, especially in the South. King made good use of his network of support as he reached down to help his unfortunate brothers and sisters from his secure, privileged position in the black middle class.

We have already looked briefly at King's family life and the secure foundation it provided him in early childhood. Now we will observe his intellectual and spiritual growth in those years of preparation in his late teens and early twenties. These were mainly years of academic preparation, though there was also some important advancement in the practice of ministry. Who King was and became was anchored in the black church, the black college, and the South before he studied at Crozer and Boston. I am grateful especially to Lewis Baldwin for making this claim solid.

Since King and I were in the same age bracket, I had the good fortune of being mentored by some of the same black religious scholars that touched his life. In the time of our studies, there was a scarcity of black scholars in the field of religion. Several had been associated with Morehouse College or Howard University. Some, like Howard Thurman and Benjamin Mays, had served at both schools. Such scholars impacted the lives of all black theology students in the nation. King was fortunate to meet and study with Mays at Morehouse. Daddy King and Mays had a lifelong friendship. Young Martin had personal counseling sessions with Mays, who was then president of Morehouse. King was at Boston University when Thurman was the dean of the chapel there, as he had been at Howard University. Martin Jr. had the opportunity of private conversations with Thurman.

There were other outstanding Morehouse teachers, whom I knew as colleagues in my early days as a Howard University professor. I also had years of dialogue with some of these men. George Kelsey and Samuel Williams were in discussions at the annual meeting of the Institute of Religion, which met at Howard's Divinity School. It was out of this context that the university's *Journal of Religious Thought* was initiated.

King's southern upbringing in Atlanta, his family life in the black family, community, and church, provided a foundation for his future life, thought, and action. What King received at Crozer and Boston is also important, but it must be evaluated against the background of what King brought to his studies on the seminary and graduate levels. All of these experiences help us understand more fully who he became and what he was able to do in his time of witness.

His observation of his parents' lifestyle gave him a deep urge to serve humanity, but this was not associated with a call to the ministry. Instead, he considered the legal and medical professions. King had certain deep concerns that needed to be addressed. He did not see how the facts of science could be squared with religion. He revolted against the emotionalism of much of African American religion, the shouting and stamping. He observed that too many black ministers were unlettered and without adequate education for their role.

It was only after he studied with Kelsey and Mays that King developed a different view of ministry. Both men combined a deep religious faith with profound thought. He saw in their lives the ideal of what he wanted to be as a minister.

In King's senior year in college, he entered the ministry. The desire to be a minister began during his high school years. Now he felt an inescapable drive and a sense of responsibility that he could not escape. Looking back, King observed that the admiration for and the example set by Daddy King had much to do with his decision to become a minister.

At Crozer Theological Seminary, King began a serious intellectual quest for a method to eliminate social evil. He turned to an intense study of the social and ethical theories of great philosophers from the early Greeks to the present. He likewise studied many social philosophers. In this effort he discovered Walter Rauschenbusch's *Christianity and the Social Crisis*. This work made an indelible imprint on his mind. It also provided King with a theological basis for the social concerns that he felt deeply. Although he was critical of Rauschenbusch's optimism regarding the goodness of humans, he was impressed that this theologian insisted that the Christian church proclaim a gospel that deals with the whole person—not only the soul but also the body, not only the spiritual but the material.

Among the thinkers King examined was Karl Marx. His careful reading of *Das Kapital* and *The Communist Manifesto* was eye opening. He also read interpretations of the thought of Marx and Lenin. King had developed a dialectical way of thinking, influenced by Hegel. In addition to his theological study, King studied philosophy at the University of Pennsylvania. He studied philosophy at Harvard University later on. This study of philosophy disciplined his mind for critical thinking. This became evident as he examined Marxism in the form of communism. King rejected the materialism, the ethical relativism, and the political totalitarianism of communism. In the meantime, he gave equal attention to a critique of capitalism.

King saw truth and falsehood in both Marxism and capitalism from a Christian perspective. Marxism, he realized, was too collective in its view of humans, while capitalism was too individualistic. The kingdom of God, he concluded, is neither the thesis of individual enterprise nor the antithesis of collective enterprise, but a synthesis of the truths of both.

At Crozer, King heard a lecture by A. J. Muste. Until hearing this message, King was uncertain about war as a means to oppose an evil force. He was pondering if war would be preferable to surrendering to a totalitarian system. He speculated that war, though not an absolute good, might be a negative good.

King came to a crisis point in his thinking. It appeared that the Christian ethic of love was confined to individual relationships. He could not see it as the answer to social conflict. What about segregation? Is armed revolt the only solution to racial conflict?

A different message was presented in a sermon by President Mordecai Johnson of Howard University. Johnson came to Philadelphia to speak at the Fellowship House. He had just returned from India, where he had observed firsthand the results of the life and teachings of Mahatma Gandhi. King was so moved by Johnson's profound and electrifying presentation that he began a serious study of Gandhi. This was a transforming experience for King.

King graduated from Crozer in May 1951. While studying at this seminary, King had felt the desire to teach in a college or seminary. He sensed a need to specialize in a particular theological field. Philosophy was attractive to Martin. He was impressed by the writings of some faculty members at Boston University, especially Edgar S. Brightman, whose specialty was the philosophy of religion. In addition, one of King's professors at Crozer was a Boston University graduate.

King's decision to do graduate study was not fully appreciated by Daddy King. Nevertheless, he honored his son's desire for advanced study. The national standing of Daddy King as a distinguished pastor provided a network of contacts for his son. Thus, Daddy and Alberta King were able to select pastors to care for their son in other cities. The Rev. J. Pius Barbour and his wife had "adopted" Martin Jr. in Chester, Pennsylvania, while he was studying at Crozer. In Boston, the Rev. William H. Hester and his wife were selected to oversee him. Martin, therefore, enjoyed a sense of belonging in an extended family in home and church that he had known in the South. This familial nurturing aided his moral and spiritual growth.

In Boston King was able to refine his thinking, decide on the nature and location of his ministry, and enter into courtship and marriage with Coretta Scott. Both of them were from the South—he from Atlanta and she from Marion, Alabama. King's decision to pastor rather than teach theology led him to become the acknowledged spiritual leader of the civil rights movement.

CONCLUSION

In this segment of our study, we have considered the events and experiences in the lives of Bonhoeffer and King that prepared them intellectually and spiritually for the dynamic leadership they were to provide in their social-historical contexts. Our next chapter will begin to assess the early stages of their activism, which shaped their lives for the witness that followed.

4

Formative Experiences in Ministry

Neither Bonhoeffer nor King was concerned about building a "system" of theology. After completing their preliminary scholarly work, both elected to be servants in the church. They were to be social activists with a solid theological foundation.

Each theologian had to work through more than one option to reach the final decision to serve the church rather than become an academic theologian. This means that in order to understand their messages and the ordering of their lives, we need to look concisely at events and issues in their early ministries. Both theologians earned doctorates. In this chapter we will look at how they launched their postdoctoral projects of ministry.

Their essential thought will be studied in course. Here we are concerned with their respective social and historical situations and how the men were involved in the events that gave rise to their powerful witness. Both Bonhoeffer and King did their work through churches or church organizations. This gave their personal outreach a more effective structure through which to operate. Bonhoeffer became known through his relationship to the Confessing Church. King did his work through the Southern Christian Leadership Conference. The use of these institutional instruments varied in outreach and effect.

BONHOEFFER'S FORMATIVE
EXPERIENCES IN MINISTRY

Bonhoeffer's close friend at Union, Jean Lasserre, led him into the peace movement. While in the United States, the two friends, Bonhoeffer a German and Lasserre a Frenchman, traveled to Mexico to attend a peace conference.

Many scholars believe that this experience and the personal influence of Lasserre upon Bonhoeffer were the impulses behind Bonhoeffer's *The Cost of Discipleship* as well as his activities in the European peace movement.

In the fall of 1931, Dietrich served both the university and the church. He worked as a chaplain at a technical college and taught a confirmation class in a poor section of Berlin. Bonhoeffer was attracted to the world stage of church affairs, as he was involved in a relatively new organization, the World Alliance of Churches. This activity led him to Cambridge, England. His concerns brought pacifism and ecumenism together. He believed that if the churches could get together, perhaps nations could learn to live together in peace. His strong emphasis upon the church as community provided a theological basis for this outlook.

His appointment as an honorary youth secretary of the World Alliance was significant. He had the role of a coordinator of youth work. He traveled widely through Europe, mainly visiting Germany, central and northern Europe, Hungary, and Austria. These contacts would be useful to Bonhoeffer later as he opposed Hitler.

The Nazis had moved forward in Germany. By the 1930 election, they were gaining control of the political situation. Few theology students in Germany shared Bonhoeffer's opposition to the political trends in Germany. In seminaries, more than half of the candidates for ordination followed Hitler. Their professors were also on board with this outlook. Most were moved by the troubled economy. They also believed that Hitler's promise to leave the church alone was true. At the time, Hitler's attitude toward the Jews was not considered. When this became known, many changed their minds. But by then Hitler was in control and it was too late. Bonhoeffer lost his popularity at the university. He was interested in international relations and peace when Germany was preparing for war.

The Bonhoeffer family gave Dietrich firm moral support. His parents, brothers, sisters, and grandmother were anti-Nazi. They did not accept the anti-Semitism and the tone of Hitler's message and action. In a word, they did not trust Hitler.

On January 30, 1933, Hitler became chancellor of Germany. Two days later, Bonhoeffer gave a radio broadcast critical of the Führer. In his message, which was directed to young people, Bonhoeffer stated that leaders who set themselves up as gods mock God. As he was speaking, the microphone was turned off. This encounter with the Nazis initiated the events of the rest of Bonhoeffer's short life.[1]

"PUT JUSTICE IN BUSINESS"

At a later time, King reflected upon the privileges of his early life and realized how fortunate he was: "The first twenty-five years of my life were very comfortable years. If I had a problem, I could always call Daddy. Things were solved."[2]

This situation was to change as he began his tenure as pastor of Dexter Avenue Baptist Church in Montgomery, Alabama. The congregation of this church was made up of the black middle class. However, prior to King's ministry there, Vernon Johns had been pastor. Johns was a powerful preacher and advocate of social justice. A solid foundation had been laid for a ministry to the oppressed in this cradle of the Confederacy.

King organized his church to move forward in its outreach ministry, and he formed social and political committees. He immediately got involved with the NAACP, which sought better race relations through court action. He also became active in the Council on Human Relations, which sought to bring about change through education. The council was an interracial group. King saw both court action and education as necessary and productive.

When Rosa Parks was arrested for violating segregation laws on a bus in Montgomery, King was suddenly involved. E. D. Nixon, a Pullman porter involved with organized labor and state president of the NAACP, was a courageous associate who drew King into the bus dispute. In support of Parks, King was elevated to the position of key leader in what became the famous bus boycott in Montgomery. The issue drew the attention of the nation and the global community to the pattern of racial discrimination in Alabama and throughout the South.

King's position as pastor of a leading congregation led to his being elected as president of the Montgomery Improvement Association. He was well educated, a powerful orator, and a new pastor in the city. He did not have any connection with the divisions among blacks in the city. He was elected by a unanimous vote. This decision changed his life and put the quest for racial justice on a new track throughout the nation. He accepted this burden of leadership, and his wife, Coretta, backed his decision. The rest is history.

Much emphasis has been focused upon the role of Ralph Abernathy in this effort. He certainly was close to Martin for many years and gave him good support. Nevertheless, more attention should have been given to the important role of Rosa Parks, for she initiated the entire movement.

Rosa Parks was a good citizen, church worker, and activist for racial justice. She was a person of intelligence, dignity, and self-respect. She was ideal for the role assigned to her by history. She had served as secretary of the local NAACP and was one of the most respected persons in the black community. Her character and dedication to others helped to arouse a large number of blacks to participate in this effort.[3]

The bus boycott lasted for about a year. On December 20, 1956, word came to Montgomery of the decision of the U.S. Supreme Court that segregation on buses in Alabama was unconstitutional. One black bystander summed the matter up as divine intervention: "God Almighty has spoken from Washington, D.C."[4]

For more than ten years after this moral victory in Montgomery, King was the most influential leader of the black American struggle for equality in the history of the United States. This civil rights history has been reported in many works by a host of scholars. I will make reference to events in King's life and work as needed.[5]

CONCLUSION

Often the influence of charismatic persons is taken into an organizational structure for widespread and lasting effect. This trend was manifested in the activities of Bonhoeffer and King.

Bonhoeffer was involved in the ecumenical movement as a youth leader. His involvement with the Confessing Church in Germany is well known. The German Evangelical Church was divided between members of the Confessing Church who opposed Hitler and the German Christians who supported Nazism. Bonhoeffer was one of the first church leaders to take a bold position against Hitler and on behalf of all Jews, not just Jews who had been baptized into the church.

In his role as an opponent of National Socialism, Bonhoeffer was appointed director of the Confessing Church's seminary. In this position he was able to prepare young pastors to be leaders in this anti-Nazi thrust in the German churches. His role in the resistance movement will be discussed later. Here we have seen how Bonhoeffer's witness was mediated through organized structures for greater effect.

As we turn to the ministry of King, we note a similar tendency. King was drawn into the leadership of the Montgomery Improvement Association. However, the role he played in the successful bus boycott initiated a church-based opposition to racism that has never ceased. Beyond this thrust against segregation, King organized and led the Southern Christian Leadership Conference, which became a national body and was effective beyond his short life.[6]

As we look back on the organizations that extended the missions of Bonhoeffer and King, there are high points and low ebbs in the effectiveness of the movements and organizations initiated by their dynamic leadership, but we must take note of what these institutional outlets accomplished.

On Sunday, September 8, 2003, I was a visitor at the Nassau Presbyterian Church in Princeton, New Jersey. The pastor spoke on "Empty Words." His text was taken from the book of James, chapter 2. This message moved me greatly. It was as if the preacher was speaking to me personally. During the week I had been reflecting on the life and thought of Bonhoeffer and King. Knowing that Bonhoeffer was Lutheran was well upon my mind. Martin Luther referred to the book of James as a "straw epistle" and wanted it deleted from the New Testament. King also spoke often about ministers in the South, black as well as white, who opted for faith but had little to say about works. But in this text and sermon, there is an obvious point of agreement for both theologians that "faith without works is dead." Personal faith has its place for both, but their greatness is expressed most in their "public theology." The passage in James provides an ideal biblical foundation for our study.

In part 2, we will explore issues and ideas that played a key role in the minds of our theologians. We will make use of this exploration as we discuss "truth and power" in the final part of this study.

PART II

Minds in the Making

5

Major Theological Resources

Part 1 of the present study introduced the early life and development of Bonhoeffer and King. Here we move into the middle stage of the lives of these two theologian-activists. It is logical that their "mid-life" would come earlier than usual since they both were martyred at age thirty-nine. This period was no more than a decade, and it began for each man when he was in his mid-twenties. Being aware of the possible early termination of his earthly life through violence, King made a significant observation: he would focus upon the quality of life. Bonhoeffer and King demonstrated for us that one could make a lasting contribution to humanity with a short life dedicated to a worthy cause.

As a Lutheran, Bonhoeffer was much influenced by Martin Luther. One of Bonhoeffer's principal professors at the University of Berlin, Karl Holl, was a noted Lutheran scholar. I will not give much attention to that influence upon Bonhoeffer at this juncture. Instead, I will have more to say about this in part 3, when we look at political theology in Bonhoeffer and King.

Now we are concerned about the powerful influence of Karl Barth upon Bonhoeffer in important aspects of the young theologian's thought and action. There was a considerable age difference between Bonhoeffer and Barth. Barth was forty-five when Bonhoeffer was only twenty-five years old. This means that Barth had passed the stage in his life that Bonhoeffer was just beginning. Nevertheless, the impact of Barth upon Bonhoeffer was important and deserves our attention.

Many years ago I listened to a lecture on Greek religious thought by Professor John Baillie at New College, Edinburgh University. Baillie spoke of a work of art he had observed in Rome that showed the images of Plato and Aristotle. The two philosophers walked together. Plato pointed up to heaven, but

Aristotle pointed down to earth. As I reflected upon the relation between Bonhoeffer and Barth, I was reminded of Baillie's illustration at the beginning of
his lecture.

Bonhoeffer met Karl Barth soon after he returned from his first trip to the
United States. He wanted to spend as much time as possible in Bonn before
the end of the semester. Erwin Sutz, a fellow student at Union Seminary in
New York who had studied with Barth, introduced Bonhoeffer to Barth. Bonhoeffer spent three weeks in a seminar with Barth on that occasion. On July
23, 1931, Barth invited Bonhoeffer to dine with him. Bonhoeffer was
delighted. The younger theologian observed that talks with Barth were much
more illuminating than reading his books.

In Barth's seminar, Bonhoeffer quoted from Luther "that the curses of the
godless are sometimes better to God than the hallelujahs of the pious."[1] This
statement was a delight to Barth and led him to take special note of this young
scholar.

During the next several years, these two theologians met and exchanged letters. They agreed on some things but disagreed on others. Ethics and ecclesiology were areas of divergence. Nevertheless, Bonhoeffer was grateful that
Barth guided his thoughts in a helpful manner.[2] Barth was open to questions,
entertained objections, pressed for directness, and did not seek agreements
with his own theology. Bonhoeffer found Barth to be an excellent dialogue
partner. In their future conversations, there was complete frankness. Sometimes there was complete disagreement also.

Bonhoeffer had difficulties with the inner circle of Barth's disciples. He was
considered "an unknown stranger." But a friend of Sutz's was cordial and provided Bonhoeffer with Barth's lecture notes for private study. The frequent
meetings with Barth continued until Bonhoeffer left for England in 1933.

In 1932, Barth visited Berlin and delivered an address titled "Theology and
Contemporary Mission." There was a heated debate reflecting a nationalistic
animosity against dialectic thinkers. Members of the faculty of the University
of Berlin and church leaders were present. This session reflected the tension
brewing in theological, political, and church circles.[3]

Barth had not examined Bonhoeffer's earliest documents of substance, San-
torum Communio and Act and Being. He knew nothing of Bonhoeffer's reservations on transcendental philosophy or Bonhoeffer's approach against Barth's
description of revelation. He was not aware of Bonhoeffer's ecclesiological
suggestions, nor of his antipathy to the incapax infinity (humanity's incapacity
for the infinite), nor of Barth's passionate protest against allowing room for
reflection in the act of faith and other matters. Bonhoeffer rejected Barth's
assertion that revelation is beyond existence.[4]

Barthians encountered Bonhoeffer only upon the release of *The Cost of Discipleship*. Hence, they were not aware of much of his early thought. In 1929, Bonhoeffer had been very outspoken in his criticism of Barth.

Bethge sets the stage for a fuller understanding of the relationship between Barth and Bonhoeffer in this manner: Barth had left the pulpit for the lectern. His theological questions arose from his experiences as preacher and pastor. The preacher in him sought the systematician (the theologian). He sought to rescue the majesty of God that had been squandered from the pulpit. He spoke of the wholly other, the remote and unapproachable God. Barth pondered how to avoid making an unholy concept in the concrete reality.

Bonhoeffer, on the other hand, came from a predominately academic environment, though he had long aspired to the pulpit. Bonhoeffer was a systematician searching for the preacher. Bonhoeffer wanted to preserve the majesty of God, whom he feared would be cheapened in the pulpit. He wanted to proclaim God in the concreteness of a grace-filled commandment. Still a theologian in mindset, Bonhoeffer was now a preacher pondering the authority and credibility of his proclamation. Old questions were fading and new questions were emerging. He faced the problems of ethics.

Barth had regarded empirical human activity, whether faith or obedience, as God's activity. Bonhoeffer wanted to ascribe something to human effort as well. Barth had pointed to the eschatological limitation of obedience. Barth seemed too cautious to Bonhoeffer, and Bonhoeffer appeared too impatient for Barth. For the sake of his eschatology, Barth described ethics as being mere "pointers" or "demonstrations." Bonhoeffer viewed Barth's position as an inadequate basis and context for the proclamation of the commandments. The more deeply Bonhoeffer became involved in church work and the ecumenical movement, the more urgent were the questions he posed to the Barthian position. He asked, Is it possible to proclaim concrete commandments through the church?

What about authority in the church? The church, as he viewed it, was unable to utter concrete commandments. Does this weakness lie in its essence? Or does this insufficiency lie in the decay and loss of substance? Bonhoeffer was also concerned about false authorities. For example, theologians such as Althaus and Brunner saw the authority for the proclamation of the commandments in the "office" of the church or in the "orders of creation." For a period, Bonhoeffer responded to this crucial issue through "a qualified silence."[5] He was later to assert, "The Barthian view of ethics as 'demonstration' rules out all concrete ethics and ethical principles. Proclaiming the concrete Christ always means proclaiming him in a concrete situation."[6]

Through this discussion we can see major threads of Bonhoeffer's thought taking shape. The sociality of the church as viewed by Bonhoeffer in his early research is evident. There is also an emphasis upon concreteness in an active ethic. Human freedom and responsibility in ethical thought and action is implied.

Let us look at one other matter that provoked a profound disagreement between Bonhoeffer and Barth. This has to do with the nature of the freedom of God as it relates to revelation. The nature of revelation involves our understanding of the nature of God and God's salvific relation to humans as well. Bonhoeffer states his case with clarity:

> In revelation it is not so much a question of the freedom of God—eternally remaining within the divine self, aseity—on the other side of revelation, as it is of God's coming out of God's own self in revelation. It is a matter of God's *given* word, the covenant in which God is bound by God's own action. . . . God is free not from human beings, but for them. Christ is the word of God's freedom. God is present, that is, not in eternal non-objectivity, but—to put it quite provisionally for now—"havable," graspable in the word within the church. Here the formal understanding of God's freedom is countered by a substantial one.[7]

Bonhoeffer ascribes a social and historical dimension to revelation. Revelation happens in the community of faith. God's freedom has woven itself into a this-worldly community of faith. This is exactly that which manifests what God's freedom is. God binds God's self to human beings.[8]

≈≈≈≈≈≈≈≈

We now turn to Martin Luther King Jr. and the major intellectual influences upon his life and thought.

King was an eclectic thinker. He had a fertile mind and examined many ideas and movements. His philosophical studies prepared him to compare and contrast ideas. Even though his doctorate was in theology, he began his graduate work at Boston University under Edgar Brightman, a philosopher of religion. He also studied philosophy at the University of Pennsylvania and at Harvard University. Hegelian logic helped to shape his entire perspective on reality. He had a mind disciplined by the study of philosophy, and he used its perspectives in essays, lectures, and sermons. One can observe the thesis/antithesis/synthesis reasoning in much of his thinking. I shall say more about this as we examine his political theology.

As the son of a leading pastor in Atlanta, King was influenced by several African American religious scholars. Benjamin E. Mays, George Kelsey, and Howard Thurman were among those from the black community who impacted his life during his college days. These thinkers combined experience of the world of black people and a liberal theological education. This study will give much attention to the foundation of King's life, thought, and action that is anchored in the black religious experience—in family, church, and community.

King's advanced scholarship was developed in seminaries and universities outside of the South. As one who shared the same experience at the same time, I can affirm the fact that blacks who sought advanced study were forced to go northward to seize this opportunity. King's mentors had done this and so did King himself. He took the experiences he had had in Atlanta with him to Crozer and Boston. There he refined, polished, and deepened his thought for a life of witness in the cause of justice for black people in particular and humankind in general.

Due to his privileged background, King had a robust optimism regarding human progress. In spite of his southern exposure to racism in the form of segregation, he had a liberal outlook toward life and the human condition. The social gospel of Walter Rauschenbusch had an immediate appeal. This theologian combined a social consciousness with a liberal view of human nature. The encounter with Reinhold Niebuhr, however, was a necessary jolt to this optimism. Niebuhr's ethical realism made King aware of the depths of human sinfulness in the form of pride. Niebuhr also made him aware of the need for grace to overcome social sins as well as personal ones. The encounter with Niebuhr's theological ethics urged King to seek a means of confronting collective evil in human relations. This, in King's view, was a necessary corrective for Rauschenbusch's optimism regarding the human condition.[9]

In his search for a place to stand, King encountered Nietzsche, Marx, and Gandhi, among others. It was the movement known as personalism that made the most lasting impression upon King's mind. Personalism was to be linked with Gandhi's nonviolent ethic as a means to oppose the evils of racist oppression. We will examine Gandhi's ideas later in King's political theology. At this time, we will give our attention to personalism.

Personalism, as presented to King by Professor George Davis of Crozer (a Boston University graduate), attracted his attention. When he had finished his pastoral studies, King was already somewhat knowledgeable of Boston personalism. In selecting a graduate program, King had considered two other schools. Yale was his first choice, but he was not accepted there. He applied for admission to the University of Edinburgh and was accepted there, but perhaps for family reasons, he chose not to attend. The distance from his parents may have been a factor. Furthermore, additional study did not sit well with Daddy King. He thought that his son was already well qualified to pastor. Nevertheless, when Daddy King realized that Martin was determined, he relented and gave full support to this additional study.

Martin went to Boston to study under Edgar Brightman, in the field of philosophy of religion. Brightman was the specialist in personalism at Boston at that time. Thus, King went to Boston in clear pursuit of a greater knowledge of personalism. In time, King would not only become well informed of this movement of thought, but he would also transform it and use it in his program of social action.[10]

King began his study under Brightman, but Brightman died in 1953. Thereafter, Harold DeWolf became King's major advisor. Therefore, DeWolf continued King's orientation in this program of thought. There was much compatibility between this philosophy and what King knew from his African American religious background.[11]

King wrote a number of papers on the doctrine of God. He saw this doctrine as central to the Christian faith. The issue of God's personal nature was with King through his reflection on Wieman and Tillich.[12] There were two main issues raised by personalism: (1) Is God personal or transpersonal? (2) Is God omnipotent and omnibenevolent, or is God absolute in goodness and finite in power? In sum, King was attracted by the assertion concerning the personal God of love and reason as well as the emphasis on the objective moral order, moral laws, and the inherent dignity of human personality.

According to King, personality in God is theomorphic, not anthropomorphic. It is in God, not in human beings, that we encounter the essence of what it means to be a person. Even though our knowledge of human personality gives us a clue to the meaning of "person," the standard of "person" is found in God, who is the absolute and perfect person. "Person" essentially means self-consciousness and self-direction. Concerning this position, King refers to the theology of Albert Knudson and Thomas Aquinas.

As King discussed the meaning of "person," he made good use of it in his project for social justice. He drew out the implications of the meaning of this idea for human beings in their understanding of self and others. It asserted the belief in an objective moral order and the need for community. All these crucial concerns stem from the assertion that God is personal.

Rufus Burrow is correct, I believe, in asserting that King was both a metaphysical and an ethical personalist. That is, he believed in a personal God who is the ground of all things, and he was a staunch believer in the sacredness of all persons.[13]

There was divergence among Boston personalists on the concept of God. Their differences were not over the existence of God but the nature or character of God. The difference was also between the philosophers (i.e., Brightman) and the theologians (i.e., DeWolf). King identified with the theologians. King could not conceive of God as limited in power, in spite of the existence and persistence of evil.[14]

King developed his own interpretation of personalism. Because his use of this position was tested in the freedom movement for African Americans, it took on a special character. For King, the biblical tradition in the black church supported the dignity of persons inherent in the concept of the image of God.[15]

King's designation of personalism is "theistic." He juxtaposed his view of personalism with the "atheistic" personalism of John M. E. McTaggert.[16] According to King, "person" is prominent both metaphysically and ethically. The worth of the individual does not lie in the measure of intellect, racial origin, or social position. It is based upon one's relatedness to God. God, through creating humans in the image of God's self, has bestowed upon humans equal worth.

Personalism, as King understood it, believes in a personal God who is creator and sustainer of the created order. In personalism, he found metaphysical grounding for the biblical claim that humans live and move and have their being in a God who is infinite, loving, caring, responsive, righteous, and just. The universe is under the guidance of this personal, loving creator God. God, according to King, is a personal being of matchless power and infinite love.

Personalism advocates freedom in persons. To be a person is to be free. A person is an agent capable of acting for good or evil. Persons have the characteristic of self-determination. This assertion has important implications for the ethical and political freedom of persons in the world. It implies that we ought to be willing to assert, protect, and defend essential freedoms.

King insists that it is in the nature of persons to be free. Freedom implies at least three things: (1) the capacity to be self-directed; (2) the ability to make decisions; and (3) responsibility for one's decisions and actions. Anything that threatens one's freedom is a threat to one's personhood. Without freedom, neither morality nor knowledge is possible.[17]

Personalism conceives of reality as thoroughly social, relational, and communal. The individual never experiences complete selfhood in isolation. The self finds fulfillment in interaction with other selves and in communication with other persons. Here we encounter the insights from our African roots. Here King also anticipates his concept of the "beloved community."[18]

Burrow correctly designates King's view, I believe, as "personal communitarianism." Just as the individual owes duties to the community, so does the community owe duties to the individual. Nevertheless, King seems to imply that the individual rather than the community has the right of way.

King went beyond his teachers in defining and applying personalism.[19] He certainly mined the school of personalism for all it was worth. He road-tested this point of view in his freedom activities. Furthermore, his personalism developed and matured in a hostile environment and against all odds. King employed personalism in a situation in which he, his family, and all other blacks were victims of racism. Burrow writes, "What King learned about human dignity, the need for self-love, cooperative endeavor, he learned from the Bible, from behavior molded by his parents and grandparents and from what he knew of the Black struggle since the time of slavery."[20]

King's personalism was fused with activism. Ministry was a vocation to which a pastor is called by God. King took this conviction as his own. Though King had mastered the concept of metaphysical personalism, he was fundamentally a "social-activist-personalist."[21] He spent his entire ministerial career applying personalistic principles to practical solutions for the problems of racism, economic exploitation, and militarism. The meaning of King's personalism was worked out in the struggle for dignity and justice, rather than in the relative comfort of the classroom or a cozy study. From Montgomery to Memphis, he lived under the threat of death. His personalism was the most vibrant and relevant of the varieties of personalism during the thirteen years of his ministry. The ripple effects of his witness remain with us.

In this chapter we first examined the relationship between the thought of Bonhoeffer and Barth. In my judgment, this relationship is fundamental in our understanding of the mindset of Dietrich Bonhoeffer as a theologian. The similarity and the difference between them casts light upon our understanding of Bonhoeffer's thought and action.

Boston personalism had a similar impact upon the life and witness of Martin Luther King Jr. I have attempted to show how King's encounter with personalism at Boston University built upon his anchor in the black experience. The metaphysical understanding of personalism refined the personalism he encountered growing up in a black family, church, and community in the South. King later used personalism in an effective manner in his quest for social justice.

The common ground for the thought of Bonhoeffer and King can be gathered up in these words from the Lord's Prayer:

> Thy kingdom come,
> Thy will be done,
>   On earth as it is in heaven.
>   Matt. 6:10

6

Race and Ethnicity

In studying Bonhoeffer and King, it is obvious that each of these activist church theologians opposed racism. Racism and anti-Semitism are similar. They are collective forms of evil. Both are forms of oppression in which one group of people dehumanizes another group of people and deprives them of their dignity. The oppressed groups are robbed of their freedom and in some cases their lives are imperiled. The plights of blacks in the United States and Jews in Nazi Germany represent sterling examples of racism and "ethnic cleansing."

Both racism and anti-Semitism have a long history. Blacks in the United States live in the shadow of slavery, which goes back about four hundred years. The scars of this evil system still affect the souls of blacks and whites in this country. Anti-Semitism has been a collective evil that has followed the Christian movement through more than 2,000 years. Nazism did not create anti-Semitism; it made use of this form of oppression that was ingrained in religious and social institutions.[1]

The word "ethnic" comes from the Greek word *ethnikon*, which means "foreign" or "national." It relates to a community with common mental, religious, or cultural traits. This may be illustrated by comparing Anglo-Saxons and Jews. Although the two groups may share the same racial characteristics, they each bear cultural and religious traits that are distinct.

The situation that Bonhoeffer encountered was on the borderline. It seemed to involve both race and ethnicity. This illustrates why racism and anti-Semitism often show up in the same place and at the same time in the United States as well as in Hitler's Germany. In this study, racism will be used frequently to cover both situations. In fact, Bonhoeffer's observations on racism in the United States deepened his understanding of the oppression of the Jews in Nazi Germany. We will examine more fully the issues raised by the "Aryan clause" and the "Jewish question" in part 3. Nevertheless, the oppression of the Jews will be introduced here.

The full force of racial and ethnic discrimination was unleashed upon the Jews by Hitler. Hitler used the history of anti-Semitism in the Christian movement and emerging German nationalism to dehumanize the Jews. Millions perished because of Hitler's carefully orchestrated racial policies.

By 1933, Hitler had been able to sell his program to the German people. He felt that the only way to ensure the preservation of nationalism was to define or dictate what to think and do. Hitler divided the populace into three categories: the fighters, the lukewarm, and the traitors.[2] This segregation plan was to be adopted in the schools, which he saw as "the seedbed for the coming generation." Young children were to be thoroughly immersed in his insidious doctrine of hate. The flying of the swastikas and the shouts of "Heil" began a ripple that became a wave unleashing death and destruction everywhere it fell.

Hitler found repugnant the aspirations of the Jews to become truly German. He was an ardent foe of Zionism. He even feared a separate Jewish state might emerge within Germany. His fears were racist and ethnic at once. He wrote, "Soon, this apparent fight between Zionists and liberal Jews disgusted me; it was unreal throughout, based on lies, and little suited to the generally accepted high moral standard and purity of this race."[3]

Hitler disliked Jews on racial, cultural, and moral grounds. In the eleventh chapter of *Mein Kampf*, Hitler seeks to totally disparage the dignity of Jews. There he refers to their "shame culture" and refers to them as "apes" and "parasites." According to Hitler, every social ill that beset the Germans could be attributed to the Jews. In the face of this hateful ideology that Hitler sold to the German people, Bonhoeffer's willingness to make a common cause with Jews stands out in bright relief.

But we are faced with another difficulty. Bonhoeffer was a Lutheran who had been indoctrinated into this Reformed tradition as a pastor-theologian. Martin Luther himself was anti-Semitic in thought and attitude. In 1543, Luther published a tract, *Concerning the Jews and Their Lies*. In this work he depicted the Jews as poisoners, ritual murderers, usurers, as devils incarnate, and parasites on Christian society.[4] The seed of hatred nurtured by Luther reached its horrible climax in the Third Reich. The "German Christians," during Bonhoeffer's period, showed themselves to be particularly receptive to Nazi anti-Semitism.

It is fortunate that Bonhoeffer was an independent thinker. We have seen that he was greatly influenced by Karl Barth, a Reformed theologian. In addition, he was deeply involved with the ecumenical movement. Bonhoeffer was as much an ethicist as he was a theologian. As an ethicist, he carefully thought out his own views and course of action.

Many members of Bonhoeffer's family held close ties with Jews. Bonhoeffer himself had close friends who were Jews. The robust humanism in Bonhoeffer's family heritage kept him from dehumanizing the Jews.

In 1977, Eberhard Bethge, Dietrich's close friend and biographer, published an article explaining Bonhoeffer's close ties with Jews. Bethge pointed out that Bonhoeffer attended Berlin High School, where "half of his classmates were Jewish." His brother-in-law, husband of his twin sister, Sabine, was Jewish. Another close friend, Franz Hildebrandt, was a Jewish-Christian pastor. Dietrich's grandmother, Julie, was a strong supporter of the Jewish people.[5]

Bonhoeffer's experience with racism in the United States made him sensitive to this form of oppression and the damage it causes to the oppressed and the oppressor alike. Later we will explore this influence with more precise information. I mention it here as one factor that heightened his sensitivity vis-à-vis the persecution of Jews in Nazi Germany.

Bonhoeffer clearly had compassion for the Jews and their suffering. He was one of the few who spoke out on their behalf. He spoke on behalf of all Jews, not only those who professed to be Christian. This courageous act eventually cost him his life.

We turn now to Martin Luther King Jr. and his opposition to racism in the form of segregation. Racism is America's "national sin." There is no part of the United States where racism does not exist. The roots of racism are in the tradition of slavery. Slavery, like anti-Semitism, has an ancient past. In the United States, it goes back about four hundred years. Several European countries sponsored the slave trade that reached the United States. The British were not only settlers in this country; they introduced slavery for economic advantage.[6]

Racism was used as a moral justification for the practice of slavery. Some who professed the Christian faith were troubled by the practice of enslaving other human beings, of denying them their basic human rights and treating them like property. Racist philosophies emerged that insisted that African Americans were less human than whites. This provided a type of salve to the conscience that made it easier for this brutal and inhumane system to continue.

Even though legalized slavery ended in 1865, blacks still live in its shadow. The influence of slavery is intergenerational; it is transmitted through the various institutions of society. King was correct when he spoke of "unconscious racism." Racism in the United States is still alive and well. In spite of moral and legal efforts by persons of goodwill from various backgrounds, racism has never been uprooted from U.S. society.[7]

In 1967 King made the following statement about racism:

> Racism is a philosophy based on a contempt for life. It is the arrogant
> assertion that one race is the center of value and object of devotion,
> before which other races must kneel in submission. It is the absurd
> dogma that one race is responsible for all the progress of history and
> alone can assure the progress of the future. Racism is total estrangement.
> It separates not only bodies but minds and spirits. Inevitably it descends
> to inflicting spiritual or physical homicide upon the out-group.[8]

George Kelsey, one of King's teachers at Morehouse, has described racism
as a religion and a form of idolatry:

> Racism as a faith is a form of idolatry, for it elevates a human factor to
> the level of the ultimate. The god of racism is the race, the ultimate
> center of value. . . . For the racist, race is the final point of reference
> for decision and action, the foundation upon which he organizes his
> private life, public institutions and public policy, and even his religious
> institutions. . . . When the racist is also a Christian, which is often the
> case in America, he is frequently a polytheist.[9]

King pointed out that the system of slavery had the endorsement of many
white clergymen, who used parts of the Bible to claim the superiority of one
race and the inferiority of another. He referred to this as a blasphemy and
heresy. The greatest blasphemy, according to King, was that whites ended up
making God a partner in the exploitation of blacks.[10]

As with most blacks, King's opposition to segregation was based upon personal experience as much as other factors. He had observed the impact of
racism upon his parents and also upon his children. He knew firsthand that
racism tore at one's self-respect and sense of worth as a human being. Fortunately, King learned from both his family and the black church the inherent
worth and dignity of all human beings. This truth served him well in his opposition to racism. He also opposed racism because of his affirmation that all
people bear the image of God:

> Deeply rooted in our religious heritage is the conviction that every
> man is an heir to a legacy of dignity and worth. Our Judeo-Christian
> tradition refers to this inherent dignity in the biblical term "the image
> of God." The "image of God" is universally shared in equal portions
> by all men. There is no graded scale of essential worth. Every human
> being has etched in his personality the indelible stamp of the Creator.
> Every man must be respected because God loves him.[11]

From what we have seen thus far in this chapter, we can note a fundamental
agreement between Bonhoeffer and King, namely, that racism is a problem with
psychological, sociological, and theological implications. We are also aware

that both men sided with the victims of this form of oppression and sought to put an end to the same.

We will conclude this chapter with a case study that brings racism and anti-Semitism together in the experience of Bonhoeffer. Our point of reference is Bonhoeffer's experience in America in 1930–1931.

Bonhoeffer first visited the United States at a significant time for blacks.[12] It was during the Great Depression, and many blacks were migrating from the South to the North. At the same time, the Harlem Renaissance (a flowering of black literary and musical expression) was at its peak. In addition to blacks born in the United States, there were many persons of the African Diaspora, especially from the West Indies, in Harlem.

Bonhoeffer came to Union Theological Seminary as a postgraduate fellow, having completed two doctoral programs at the University of Berlin. At this time he was "making up his mind" about faith and practice. He was a careful observer of all of his experiences outside of Germany. The American experience was enriching, but, in many ways, it was also disappointing. Bonhoeffer was turned off by the message of celebrated American preachers, such as Harry Emerson Fosdick at Riverside Church, and by what he described as "Protestantism without the Reformation." Preachers did not do justice to biblical interpretation of theological creeds, as he viewed their message. They were mainly interested in social issues. This lack was reinforced by the absence of serious theological reflection. He observed that "only in the Negro churches did he find that they spoke and heard in a Christian way of sin and grace and love toward God and the final hope."[13]

What Bonhoeffer observed in American churches has meaning today for black churches no less than for white churches. His views are prophetic and worth pondering. His four points are listed in summary form:

First, the unity of the church in both its origin and in its goal is fundamental. Where the unity of the church is forgotten as its origin, human organizations take the place of unity in Jesus Christ.

Second, there is no arrogance in claiming to be the true church of Jesus Christ. The church is a church for sinners and not only for the righteous.

Third, the unity of the church as promised is a work of the Holy Spirit, which cannot be forced by common action or theological discussion.

Fourth, American denominations have no creedal bases, while the confessional churches (of the Reformation) derive their character from the unity in the creeds. Unity in one is organization, while unity in the other is creedal.

Bonhoeffer's observations are especially timely for the present, when so many megachurches resemble big businesses rather than places where people seek to acknowledge their sin and to encounter God's grace.

Bonhoeffer befriended an African American student, Frank Fisher, from Alabama. Fisher was the one who introduced Dietrich to Harlem, which lies just beyond Union Theological Seminary. Fisher brought Bonhoeffer to the Abyssinian Baptist Church, which at the time was under the leadership of Adam Clayton Powell Sr.

After attending a service at Riverside Church, during which Bonhoeffer heard a sermon addressed to upper-middle-class members, he was able to assess the differences between the two situations. Bonhoeffer was a keen observer of the racial problems in Harlem. Thus, the worship and preaching in black churches made a great impression upon him. He was sensitive to the plight of the oppressed blacks in Harlem and elsewhere in the United States.[14]

Many writers on Bonhoeffer have mentioned in passing the experience that Bonhoeffer had in Harlem. Here I will attempt to draw more attention to that encounter. In order to do so, I need to stress the role of Frank Fisher as well as the climate of human relations at Abyssinian Baptist Church.

Bonhoeffer taught Sunday school at that church. It is also reported that he preached there on a few occasions. He entered into fellowship with this black congregation. He must have gotten to know the pastor in this context. Some of the ideas and language Powell used in preaching come up in Bonhoeffer's own literary work. Most of all, Bonhoeffer's experiences in Harlem and in this church informed his witness in Nazi Germany.

This Harlem congregation has a special history and mission for the liberation of blacks. The political activities of Adam Clayton Powell Jr. are well known.[15] However, it was during the pastorate of Adam Clayton Powell Sr. that Bonhoeffer experienced the powerful witness against racism that informed his theology and ministry.

Being in Harlem during the revival of black culture in literature and music had a great impact on Bonhoeffer. He read James Weldon Johnson's *Autobiography of an Ex-Colored Man*, W. E. B. DuBois's *Souls of Black Folk*, and the poetry of Langston Hughes and Countee Cullen.[16] He was also fascinated by black music in Harlem. Trained as a classical pianist, he began to learn the improvisation of jazz, the contingency pathos of the blues, and the liberation of black spirituals. This influence surfaced in his theological reflection. He was later to apply a musical rather than a biblical or ethical metaphor to the doing of theology. Theology, he observed, is neither a neat harmony nor a mere symphony, but polyphony. Polyphony is a musical style in which two or more different melodies come together in a satisfying way. According to Bonhoeffer, the church's *canticus firmus*, its fixed traditional melody, must remain in place and yet invite the innovation of other voices (or points of view). This outlook is evident in his *Ethics* and *Letters and Papers from Prison*.[17]

Franklin Fisher grew up in Birmingham, Alabama. He was the son of a black Baptist minister who was dean of the theology department at Alabama's Selma University. Frank earned his BA at Howard University. Howard was connected to the Harlem Renaissance through some of its professors, among them Alain Locke in philosophy and Sterling Brown in literature. Fisher came to New York to study theology but also to explore Harlem. He took his new German friend with him. As we have seen, the Abyssinian Church was an ideal location from which to get a good experience of Harlem. Fisher introduced Bonhoeffer to both its sacred and secular dimensions. There Bonhoeffer saw racism in full force and hated what he observed.

Bonhoeffer became a sensitive critic of American racism, which deepened his critique of German anti-Semitism. He discussed this problem with his brother, Karl-Friedrich, who was studying at Harvard University at the time. His older brother, a physicist, concluded that the problem of racism in the United States was so terrible that he could never imagine raising a family in the United States. Dietrich agreed with him. They both concluded that racism was the American problem for any person of conscience. He could not, at that time, anticipate the full force of race hatred that would assume and overtake the German people in church and society. Nevertheless, it was in New York that this German Lutheran theologian first began to truly understand the issues of racism and nationalism as serious theological problems.[18]

Fisher asked Bonhoeffer to go back to Germany and tell his people about the suffering of American blacks. There is concrete evidence that Bonhoeffer carried this message back with him. He worked and lived in the slums with wayward youth, and he made frequent use of black spirituals. His passion for the liberation of the oppressed in his home country is evidence of how his encounter with racism in Harlem impacted his life, his theology, and his witness on behalf of the Jews.[19]

I am often asked whether Bonhoeffer influenced King. So far as I know, he did not. It does not appear that King's professors were advocates of Bonhoeffer's thought. The follow-up question is why I, an African American, am so impressed with Bonhoeffer. There are at least two reasons. First, I was introduced to Bonhoeffer by Professor John Baillie when I was in the PhD program at Edinburgh University. Baillie was a philosophical theologian who had taught Bonhoeffer philosophical theology at Union Theological Seminary. Baillie insisted that Bonhoeffer should be studied and taken seriously. For this reason I was not impressed by the "death of God" interpretation of Bonhoeffer. Second, when I entered into conversation with liberation

theologians, Bonhoeffer emerged as an important theologian who identified
with the oppressed.

Bonhoeffer and King held many things in common during their years of
study. Bonhoeffer and King shared much of Euro-American thought. For
example, Reinhold Niebuhr had a seminal influence on both theologians. The
social gospel movement impacted both also. Bonhoeffer appeared somewhat
full of pride when he taught a course at Union on Karl Barth. He is reputed
to have asked the American students to forget all they had learned as he interpreted the theology of Barth. Our review of his encounter with the American
situation indicates that his life was greatly transformed by his year of study and
reflection on the American experience.

If King shared the Euro-American experience with Bonhoeffer, Bonhoeffer learned much through his encounter with the African American culture and
religion. Bonhoeffer had an in-depth encounter with black culture and religion in Harlem. Bonhoeffer, as a gifted musician, was attracted to the spirituals, which he used in his ministry in Germany. The spirituals are significant
because they capture "the tragic soul life" of blacks from slavery to the present. They chronicle the history of black suffering and the faith and hope that
nurtured this people throughout their history.

7

Love in Action

The Christian doctrine of love is important for both Bonhoeffer and King. This virtue is not easy to define, yet it is at the heart of the Christian message of forgiveness and redemption. Love is like the "tie that binds" Christians to each other in fellowship. Love reaches out to all persons in the family of humankind. Therefore, these two church theologians gave some serious attention to the love ethic in the Christian movement.

Love encompasses the whole of God's creative and redemptive action. The entire history of redemption can be placed under this virtue. In Christian theology, love involves many subjects: grace, election, reconciliation, justification, and sanctification on God's part. On the human side of the spectrum it involves gratitude, reverence, loyalty, and responsibility.[1]

Love is an essential concept and virtue in Bonhoeffer's theology from beginning to end. In the early years of his teaching and ministry (1927–1933), Bonhoeffer was concerned about the nature and practice of love. Love, according to Bonhoeffer, was present in humanity's primal state. Love provided communion between "I and thou." This community of mutual love was one of ruling and serving. God ruled over humankind by limitless serving. Among humans, this changed to mutual service under the rule of God. When sin entered through the fall, community was broken, and love of self replaced love of others. From this followed humankind's autonomy, estrangement, will to dominate, and bondage of self.

In the midst of this fallenness, God acts to bring about reconciliation—the Word becomes flesh! The love of God revealed in Jesus Christ's life, crucifixion, and resurrection is brought to humans by the Holy Spirit.[2]

According to the New Testament, Bonhoeffer asserts, love is defined in two distinct ways: in a positive sense, as the love of God that is revealed in Jesus

Christ, and negatively, as the love of ourselves. We must not start, however, from our love for God or for humans, but from the love of God, which reveals itself in the cross of Christ, in our justification, and in the founding of the church. The love of God also reveals and redeems us from our egoistic attitude toward ourselves. According to Bonhoeffer, the moral command to love is not specifically Christian, but the reality of love is present only in Christ and his church. Christian love has for him a special meaning.

We may now summarize Bonhoeffer's view of Christian love as follows:

1. Christian love is not a human possibility. It is not to be equated with humanitarian ideas of affection, sympathy, or eroticism.

2. Christian love is possible only through faith in Christ and through the work of the Holy Spirit. We are to surrender our will to Christ and make no claim on God or our neighbor.

3. Christian love, as an act of the will, is purposive. The will of God is that the other person(s) be subject to God's lordship. How to carry out this aim varies according to circumstances and must be perceived by each individual by himself or herself.

4. The Christian loves the real neighbor. This is a significant point. The Christian loves another human, not because of his or her attractiveness but because that person acts as a "thou" and makes the Christian experience God's claim in this "thou." In other words, love is not directed to God in the neighbor but to the concrete "thou." Bonhoeffer's critique of Karl Barth on this point is useful. Barth had suggested in the *Epistle to the Romans* that we are to love "the One" in the neighbor. No, protests Bonhoeffer, we are not to love God in the neighbor, but the neighbor in himself or herself. Humans are of supreme significance in themselves. We love others by placing our entire self at their service. This has an individual and social reference. We are not to love the neighbor in God's place or to love God in the neighbor. Instead, we are to put the neighbor in our own place and to love the neighbor rather than ourselves.

5. Christian love knows no limits. It seeks the realization of God's lordship. God's commands to love our neighbor must be obeyed without reservation.[3]

The church is a community in which persons are not only together (that is, *with* each other) but *for* each other. Being for one another is actualized through an act of love. This can be expressed in three ways: active work for our neighbor, prayers of intercession, and mutual granting of the forgiveness of sins in God's name. All these expressions of love are accomplished by abandoning oneself for the neighbor, being ready to do and bear everything in the neighbor's stead, and, if necessary, sacrificing oneself (acting vicariously) for the neighbor.[4]

John Godsey summarizes Bonhoeffer in *The Communion of Saints*, as follows: "Love is not only the life-principle of the church but also the aim of the Kingdom of God. God's will . . . is to build a kingdom of persons in which

God's love conquers and rules. Thus the divine love is both a means to an end and an end in itself; it serves to realize the community and reigns in it."[5]

Bonhoeffer observes that the commandment to love is not exclusively Christian. At the same time, there is something new about Jesus' commandment to love. According to Bonhoeffer, the newness lies in who said it. The One who said it is able to set us free for ethical action, to place humans before God, and to reveal the divine will.[6]

Creation and Fall is an interpretation of Genesis 1–3 in which Bonhoeffer stresses the nature and purpose of love. God's love is manifested in what God created before the creation of humans, yet God does not reveal God's self in that aspect of creation.[7] In the human creature, God lovingly creates his image on earth. Humans are like the Creator in that they are free. Freedom is a relationship between two persons. Being free means "being free for the other, because the other has bound me to him or her. God who is free creates humans who are free for God."[8] Elsewhere Bonhoeffer insists that "God is not free *of* man but *for* man. Christ is the Word of his freedom."[9]

In some sense, Bonhoeffer's reflection on Christian love had been theoretical until Hitler became the German leader in 1933. Nevertheless, Bonhoeffer had to ask the hard questions: How does one love the enemy? How does one love neighbors who are innocent victims of unjust racial policies? Bonhoeffer turned to thoughts of "suffering love" at this juncture. He asserted that the love of God calls humans to suffer for the oppressed.[10]

Previously, I lifted up the importance of the Sermon on the Mount for the understanding of the Christian ethic of love, especially its commandment to love one's enemies. As the oppression of the Jews and the persecution of Christians in the Confessing Church intensified, Bonhoeffer deepened his interpretation of love in such works as *The Cost of Discipleship* and *Life Together*. He had to deal with the relationship between justification and sanctification; in his Lutheran heritage, it was the problem of love and gospel. If one has faith and is saved by faith alone, does one need to be concerned about good works? How does one understand Luther? Bonhoeffer makes faith and obedience reciprocal.[11]

Bonhoeffer insists that in a spiritual community, *agape* (the selfless, redeeming love of God) abounds. The *eros* type of love is directed to the other person for the other person's sake. In the community of the Spirit, one loves the other for Christ's sake. The love that leads one to serve others has its source in Jesus Christ and his Word. Spiritual love is from above; it is from God through Jesus Christ.[12]

In Bonhoeffer's final years, he was limited in what he was able to write or say. The years between 1940 and 1943 put a damper on his "churchly" work, but increased his "worldly" work. In 1940, he became a civilian employee of the Army Military Intelligence, the Abwehr. He used this as a cover for his resistance against Hitler. Cut off from many of his family members and close friends, Bonhoeffer began work on his *Ethics*, intended as his magnum opus. Unfortunately, this work was never completed. Fragments of this material were collected and edited by his biographer, Eberhard Bethge.

One of the chapters in this work is important for our understanding of Bonhoeffer's interpretation of Christian love. The title of this chapter is "The Love of God and the Decay of the World." Bonhoeffer contrasts the disunity of the fallen world with the world recovered by the unity one finds in the New Testament. The latter unity is brought about by God's reconciling act in Jesus Christ. Love is God in God's self. Thus, to know what love truly is, we must learn its meaning from God's self-revelation, that is, from Jesus Christ.[13] We will continue to examine Bonhoeffer's views on love at the end of his life in our discussion of his political theology.

⋚⋛⋚⋛⋚⋛

King had a passionate commitment to the love ethic in his theology. In fact, love is the key concept in his worldview. It is instructive to repeat his favorite biblical passage here: "You shall love the Lord your God with all your heart, and with all your soul, and with all your mind. This is the great and first commandment. And a second is like it, You shall love your neighbor as yourself. On these two commandments depend all the law and the prophets" (Matt. 22:37–40).

King was impressed by the classical study of love by Swedish bishop Anders Nygren.[14] In many of King's lectures and sermons, he reviewed the different meanings of love discussed by Nygren. King's excitement over Nygren's study was so passionate as to appear uncritical. He might have inquired if there were other viable options. He could have considered that Nygren was Lutheran and that Luther's "two kingdoms" outlook may have imposed limitations upon a Christian ethic. Reinhold Niebuhr's critique was useful. Niebuhr suggested that *agape* has some application in individual lives but that its effectiveness in social relationships is questionable. Social relations (especially in institutions), according to Niebuhr, demand the more realistic goal of justice.[15] Niebuhr refers to the Christian love ethic as "a possible impossibility" and goes on to say that "love is always crucified in history." Since King was greatly moved by Niebuhr's realism, this pessimistic outlook must have been hard for him to assimilate. We will look critically at this problem later, but let us first consider King's position on the nature of love in the Christian ethic.

King examined Plato's dialogues to get definitions for *eros*, *philia*, and *agape*. He explains that *eros* is romantic or aesthetic love, *philia* is the reciprocal love of friendship—we love because we are loved, and *agape* is an understanding, a creative and redemptive goodwill. *Agape*, according to King's understanding, is God's love operating in the human heart. The real test case for *agape* is the love of enemies.[16]

Whereas King was impressed with Nygren's interpretation of love as a basis for self-sacrifice, as a theologian in the "black power" era, I had some reservations. I questioned King's emphasis upon unmerited suffering as being *always* redemptive. Sometimes suffering results from the absence of self-esteem. This issue surfaced among the young followers of King who began to ask why they were being treated in an inhumane manner in the quest for freedoms they deserved as human beings. After King's death, these types of questions became more critical and acute.

Furthermore, as mentioned earlier, King seemed to have followed too closely Nygren's interpretation of Christian love. If he had carefully studied the entire Bible and examined the history of doctrine, he could have found a more comprehensive understanding of Christian love.[17]

By looking, for example, at the interpretation of love by Augustine, King would have broadened and deepened his definition of love. According to Augustine, the meaning of love is determined by its object. If our attention is directed away from God, love becomes sinful. If, on the other hand, it is directed toward God, it becomes exalted. Augustine used the term *cupiditas* to describe the former and *caritas* to describe the latter. For Augustine, love for God (*amor Dei*) is the Christian ethical direction that grounds all Christian expressions of love. The love of self and of the neighbor is worthy only in God's love.

King, however, overcomes many of our theoretical concerns as his ethical theology bears fruit through action. Ervin Smith reminds us that King did not perceive love as an abstract concept only. He was interested in how the meaning and practice of love enhanced the relation of persons in community. According to King, love is concretely relevant to human social action. Love expresses itself through respect for human personality, concern for personal and social freedom for all persons, respect for the objective moral law, and consistent respect for the social or community good.[18] Smith observes: "King's most enduring contribution to Christian ethics and American social progress may be the fact that he so persistently . . . insisted upon the relevance and applicability of love to American . . . social problems."[19]

<hr>

The love ethic of Jesus and the Christian movement is fundamental for social action for Bonhoeffer and King. In this chapter we have seen the place and value of the love ethic in their thinking. More important for our reflection is the manner in which the love of God as revealed in the life and ministry of Jesus Christ informed their lives and witness for the betterment of the human family.

We have discovered common ground in Bonhoeffer and King in their search for the meaning of love for thought and action. Because of the importance of love for their lives and missions, we will be returning to the subject of love often, especially in part 3, where we will consider their political theology. Bonhoeffer sums up what it means to "love the enemy" in a manner that, in spirit at least, seems to have been shared by King:

> Love . . . shows no special favor to those who love in return. When we love those who love us, . . . we are no better than the publicans. Such love is ordinary and natural, . . . whether we are Christians or not, and there is no need for Jesus to teach us that. But he takes that kind of love for granted, and in contrast asserts that we must love our enemies. Thus he shows us what he means by love, and the attitude we must display toward it.[20]

8

Confronting Collective Evils

The reality of evil is so much a part of the witness of King and Bonhoeffer that a chapter devoted to this subject is in order. In this study thus far I have treated Bonhoeffer first, then King. This makes good chronological sense. However, King's views on "collective evil" are set forth in such an emphatic manner that I will discuss his position first. This makes good sense from a logical point of view.

Evil is something that brings sorrow, distress, or calamity. Evil can be a natural, moral, or religious experience. Evil is an experience that brings pain, especially to humans. Because of the power of thought, humans usually ask *why* when evil befalls them. Humans seek to interpret their encounters with evil, in whatever form it is experienced. The reality of evil can be personal, individual, or existential. But it can also be social, institutional, or structural.

In this chapter we will direct our attention to collective or systemic evil. From a theological perspective we cannot ignore individual sin or transgression. The two church theologians in our study are on board with the reality of human personal sinfulness. Nevertheless, they chose to confront evil as it is manifest in sinful social structures. Collective evil is more stubborn and complicated to understand and overcome than personal evil. It is subtle and difficult to detect. Nevertheless, it can do incredible harm to groups of people. We have mentioned already the harm that racism and anti-Semitism can do.

Martin Luther King Jr. is to be applauded as a privileged individual who identified with the downtrodden masses of his race. Daddy King had experienced in his youth the nightmare of racism as a sharecropper's son. Even Martin's wife, Coretta, had seen and experienced the bitter fruit of racist oppression as a child of the South (Alabama). Up until King completed his doctoral work,

his father had provided for his economic support. Due to Daddy King's
national influence, Martin had been "adopted" by an extended family in
Chester and Boston. In spite of all these advantages, he had identified so completely with a suffering race that he dedicated his life and ministry to the over-
coming of the collective evil of racism.

King's grandfather and father had demonstrated their concern for members
of their race who were poor and mistreated. Thus, from his childhood King
was sensitive to the need to uplift those persons who were in the greatest need
of dignity and freedom. His mother and grandmother also insisted that he was
just as good as anybody. At Morehouse College, he met the best personal
examples of minister-professors, who set him on the right path for racial uplift.
It was in that context that he accepted a call to minister in the church. King
saw everything he did as a fulfillment of the call to Christian ministry.

He built his education upon this solid foundation. As he studied, he kept
always in view an evil system that he wanted to confront with the hope that
life could be more human for those who were being crushed by it.

King's education moved forward on two tracks. On the one hand, he was
seeking degrees to pastor or teach. On the other hand, he was seeking to identify a philosophy and method to transform American society and free his people. This project for social transformation was later to include those who were
the victims of economic exploitation (poor whites) and those who were the victims of war.

King was excited when he read Thoreau's "On the Duty of Civil Disobedience." Thoreau had insisted that the citizens of Massachusetts should refuse
to cooperate with a system that involved them in the evils of slavery. He
opposed the mistreatment of Native Americans and the war with Mexico.
Thoreau also maintained that those who called themselves abolitionists should
withdraw their support, both in taxes and in person and property, from the
government of Massachusetts. Thoreau insisted that a creative minority could
serve the state by resisting it with the intention of improving it. He even indicated that jail is the only house in a slave state in which a free man can
abide with honor, that the demands of conscience must come before civil
obedience.[1]

King was impressed as well with the warrants to overcome collective evils in
the Sermon on the Mount. However, when he read Niebuhr's description of
social evils in *Moral Man and Immoral Society*, he was discouraged in his search
for a method to encounter and overcome a massive social evil like racism.[2]

King had been inspired by the social gospel of Walter Rauschenbusch to
such a degree that he was almost overcome by the belief in human progress that
this theologian expressed. King initially received Rauschenbusch's message in
an uncritical manner. This was supported by the wholesome experiences he had

had in family and church. This rosy view was shattered by reading Reinhold Niebuhr and by a careful look at the real racial situation in America.

Liberalism had stressed the natural goodness of humans and the power of human reason to the extent that King had gained intellectual satisfaction in this stream of thought. Reinhold Niebuhr helped King turn from the sentimentality of liberalism to recognize the complexity of social involvement and the reality of sin on every level of human existence. Niebuhr's focus was strong as he viewed collective evil. King indicates that Niebuhr sensitized him to the depths of the human potential for evil. King thus came to realize that any attempt at social transformation could not ignore this potential for evil.[3]

As King looked at collective evil, he recognized its "aggressive nature." He concluded that collective evil must, therefore, be opposed by an active expression of goodness. He saw evil as "stark, grim and colossally real."[4] King uses a biblical illustration to confirm this point. He lifts up the account of Pharaoh's resistance to the Israelites' struggle for freedom: "This tells us something about evil that we must never forget, namely, that evil is recalcitrant and determined and never voluntarily relinquishes its hold short of a persistent, almost fanatical resistance."[5]

For King, then, there is a distinct characteristic of collective evil over against personal evil. That is to say, evil as expressed through a social group is more complex than in a personal relationship. For example, persons who are kindhearted as individuals may be consumed by hate as part of a group. I have observed whites in the South who were kind and generous toward me but who would then turn bitter toward other blacks when they met them. Some would express kindness in one-on-one relations, but became irate even toward me in the presence of other whites. In most groups, persons who have high principles when taken by themselves may be directed to questionable causes as members of a group. This may be observed in church fellowship as well as in other institutions.

The other aspect of collective evil that King observed and found useful in his movement toward freedom was that collective evil is real and stubborn. It has a structure that must be resisted. Consequently, the nonviolent method that he employed had to be active rather than passive.

These and other insights King gleaned from his search for a deep understanding and engagement with collective evil served him well in his "stride toward freedom."

⊰⊱⊰⊱⊰⊱

One has to search diligently in the writings of Bonhoeffer to find a clear reading of his theoretical understanding of evil. I will now attempt to put together what I have found.

Bonhoeffer insists that the knowledge of good and evil lies at the foundation of all ethical reflection. The first task of Christian ethics is to invalidate
this knowledge. The claim to the knowledge of good and evil by humans
means to deny the origin of human beings. Humans at their origin know only
God. It is only in the unity of this knowledge of God that we know others,
things, and ourselves. We know all things only in God, and God in all things.
If we attempt to depart from our origin, by which Bonhoeffer seems to mean
our being in God's creative purpose, we know ourselves, but we no longer
know God. The knowledge of good and evil on our own means separation
from God. Only against God can we as humans know good and evil.[6] Bonhoeffer observes: "Originally man was made in the image of God, but now his
likeness to God is a stolen one. As the image of God, man draws his life entirely
from his origin in God, but the man that has become like God has forgotten
how he was at his origin and has made himself his own creator and judge."[7]

Thus, humans assume the role that God alone has as Creator. This is our
downfall. To know good and evil is to know oneself as the origin of good and
evil—the origin of an eternal choice and election. This privilege belongs to
God only. Instead of accepting the choice and election of God, the human
being desires to choose, to be the origin and election. Instead of knowing
oneself as one chosen and loved by God, one becomes like God but against
God. The result of this decision is that humans cut themselves loose from life,
from the eternal life that proceeds from the choice of God. In this situation,
humans are cut off from the unifying, reconciling life in God and delivered
over to death. We are now in disunion with God, with others, with things, and
with self.[8]

In this state of disunion with God, all knowledge is self-knowledge. The
self is now wrapped up in itself and is estranged not only from God but also
from the natural order and other persons. The result of this condition is disunion with life and law, knowledge and action, idea and reality, reason and
instinct, duty and inclination, necessity and freedom, universal and concrete,
individual and collective human experience. All vital experiences are set in a
state of conflict—truth, justice, beauty, and love come into opposition. What
Bonhoeffer is describing is the human condition, both in personal and social
relations, when humans as creatures seek to become their own creator and
alienate themselves from God, the true Creator and source of their origin.[9]

In creation, God has made humans free. In this we resemble the Creator,
who is free and is the source of our freedom. Bonhoeffer insists that we are not
just free for ourselves, but free for others also. Freedom is not a quality that
can be discovered. It is not a possession or an object. Freedom is a relationship. It is a relationship between persons. Only in relationship with the other
am I free. Freedom is the event that happens to me through the other. This

assertion, Bonhoeffer believes, is not based upon speculation. It is based upon the gospel itself. God's freedom has bound us to the divine self. God's grace becomes real only in this relationship with us. God does not will to be free for the divine self but for us humans.[10]

Bonhoeffer insists that humans are created with freedom to make decisions. We are not creatures of instinct. For him, freedom is for relationships. God is free for humans as well. Separation from God, self-idolatry, is characterized by broken relationship with God, others, and self. Here we have the foundation for a sinful, evil-ridden community. Kelly and Nelson assert:

> The rebellion-sin that darkens the light of God's creating in the image of God's son is cast by Bonhoeffer into a socio-christological context. To be created in God's image . . . implies that one is in a special relationship with God and is, thereby, placed as individual in binding social relationship with other people. . . . It is in personal and social wholeness alone that one images God.[11]

His interpretation of the fall is Bonhoeffer's explanation for sin as a broken relationship between human and God, others, and self. For Bonhoeffer, moral evil in its personal and collective manifestations harks back to the human assumption of self-creation and rejection of God's role as the Author of nature, especially as the Creator of human life. Humanity refuses to remain creature and instead succumbs to the temptation to play God.

The fall, therefore, is about our destruction of our own creatureliness. To be created in the image of God was to have been created with creaturely freedom—the freedom of one person bound to the other in responsible relationship. Once those created in God's image decide to become creators, as if they were God, the freedom-in-relationship of creatureliness is no longer possible. Wayne Floyd sums up this situation by saying that

> Bonhoeffer saw this writ large across the world around him. In a time filled with those crying out for justice from concentration camps, ghettos, and ultimately the death camps themselves, Bonhoeffer witnessed political and military machinery that encouraged people to play God with others' lives. The Fall occurred again and again, day after day—and the church was silent.[12]

We have observed that King and Bonhoeffer, each in his own way, view collective evil as real. They seek a deeper understanding of its nature in order to initiate an assault upon it for social transformation in the interest of social justice. King reflects upon the story of the exodus and the message of the prophets to lay a foundation for his witness. The love ethic of Jesus and the entire Sermon on the Mount provide biblical warrants for his understanding of collective evil. He mines extrabiblical sources as well, as we have seen.

Bonhoeffer seems to find his biblical explanation for collective evil in his interpretation of the fall and the broken relationship that stems from it. His insights are drawn from several of his writings, including *Communion of Saints*, *The Cost of Discipleship*, *Ethics*, and *Letters and Papers from Prison* as sources of his comprehensive statement on collective evil. With these thoughts before us, let us turn to the final chapter in part 2, on the influence of Gandhi on Bonhoeffer and King.

9

The Fellowship of Kindred Minds: Gandhi, Bonhoeffer, and King

At a time when we are acutely aware of the dark side of religion, it is important to be reminded of the benefits of religion to human well-being. The three religious thinkers covered in this chapter each made an enormous contribution to the uplifting of the human family. It has been a great inspiration for me to take a second look at their witness, individually and collectively.

A BRIEF BIOGRAPHICAL SKETCH OF GANDI

The religious thinkers and activities in this chapter appear chronologically. The times and places of their life experiences are crucial for understanding what they thought and the importance of their mission. With this in mind, we begin with Gandhi.

Mahatma Gandhi was born in 1869 in Porbandar, a small town on the western coast of India. His family was middle class, made up of traders and farmers. According to the scheme of the caste system then operating in Indian society, this was the *kshatriya* caste, next to the top strata of that society, the *brahmana* caste. Gandhi's father was not particularly religious, but his mother was a devout Hindu. Gandhi indicates that she was forever in his thoughts for her saintliness. As a young boy he was a rebel. He was a mediocre student, he smoked cigarettes, ate meat in defiance of his vegetarian family, and experimented with other kinds of taboos. He would steal and visit prostitutes. He married at age 13 and began what he describes as "a life of lustful indulgence." When his father died, he wasn't present due to the lustful habits he had chosen. This lustful incident left a deep stamp of inner shame and guilt that resulted in his obsession with asceticism.

Gandhi studied law in London with the intention of practicing law for the Indian government. He traveled to London in 1888 and returned to India in 1891. His experiences in London intensified his indignation toward the caste system. He went to Bombay to practice law, but his nervousness about public speaking made him a completely ineffective lawyer.[1]

In 1893 a Muslim firm invited him to take a case in South Africa. Gandhi states that in Africa he "found God." In South Africa he encountered extreme racism not only against blacks but against Indians as well. He had several personal experiences with racism. His refusal to remove his turban led to vicious criticism in the local press. During a train trip to Pretoria, a white passenger objected to his presence in his car. When Gandhi refused to leave, he was put off the train without his luggage or coat in the middle of winter. This incident left a deep mark on Gandhi; he indicates that it changed the course of his life. He was inclined to return to India after this incident, but decided to "stay and suffer." Thereafter, Gandhi began his "experiment with truth through nonviolent action."

THE ATTRACTION OF THE SERMON ON THE MOUNT

Though Gandhi was a Hindu, I consider him as a mentor to Bonhoeffer and King as Christian theologians. The reason for this will become clearer as our discussion moves forward. King confirmed this when he said, "Jesus gave me the *message*, but Gandhi gave me the *method*," speaking of nonviolent action.

Bonhoeffer was taught by notable European and American scholars. Karl Barth and Reinhold Niebuhr helped to shape his thoughts in the postdoctoral stage of his development. King was taught by African American scholars such as Mays, Thurman, and Kelsey. In addition, the personalists at Boston, especially Brightman and DeWolf, impacted his thinking. Nevertheless, Gandhi had an unusual impact upon his thinking and witness. Bonhoeffer was equally anxious to learn more about Gandhi for his own mission. This discussion will attempt to assess why Gandhi's life, thought, and action made such a deep impression upon Bonhoeffer and King, two theologian-ethicists.

All three of these religious thinker-activists were drawn to the Sermon on the Mount. We shall look first at Gandhi's attraction to the Sermon on the Mount. Gandhi himself stated his interest in this sermon:

> . . . My acquaintance with the Bible began nearly forty-five years ago,
> and that was through the New Testament. I could not then take much
> interest in the Old Testament, which I had certainly read, if only to

fulfill a promise I had made to a friend whom I happened to meet in a hotel. But when I came to the New Testament and the Sermon on the Mount, I began to understand the Christian teaching. The teaching of the Sermon on the Mount echoed something I had learnt in childhood and something which seemed to be part of my being and which I felt was being acted up to in the daily life around me.[2]

John Hick has made several useful observations concerning Gandhi that I will summarize here. Hick notes that Gandhi's ideas were always embodied in action. According to Gandhi, the function of religion is to transform human life from self-centeredness to reality-centeredness. His life was one of continuous growth in which he became increasingly dedicated to the service of the higher reality, which he thought of as Truth or God. He renounced his private ego and became a servant of humankind. He loved Truth (God) with all his heart, mind, and soul, and his neighbor as himself. He maintained this outlook amid the pressures, disturbances, ambiguities, and confusions of his involvement in liberation struggles in South Africa and then in India.

Hick points to four areas that represent Gandhi's life perspective. I believe a review of these points, which I accept as representative, will help us understand his attraction to the Sermon on the Mount. The first area is Gandhi's religious pluralism. The second is his involvement in liberation praxis. Hick observes that Gandhi was perhaps the first liberation theologian. The third area is his concern for the ecological crisis. Gandhi stressed cleanliness and purity. The fourth area is Gandhi's practice of a style of contemporary sainthood. He was a *mahatma* (Great One), because he was transparent Truth. Through his life, Truth was felt and responded to by others. The Truth that seized him also grasped others through him, making great demands on their lives.[3] Bonhoeffer and King are among those moved by Gandhi's powerful witness to Truth.

Margaret Chatterjee makes other observations that are helpful. Gandhi was from Gujarat, where Hindus, Muslims, and Jains respected each other's beliefs. The only religious conflict came from fundamentalist Christians who sought converts. Gandhi was bothered by their sinful lifestyles, as he then saw them. These Christians represented a foreign imperial power that oppressed his people. They also were beef eaters and liquor drinkers. It is noteworthy that Gandhi's mother, though a devout Hindu, was influenced by the Jains, who had a rigorous belief in the sacredness of all forms of sentient life. Gandhi's strong belief in *ahimsa* (noninjury) can be traced to this source.[4]

Gandhi was suspicious of those who were easy converts to a religion different from their own. He insisted that prayer for others should be that each be given the light needed to understand better his or her own religion. The Hindu should seek to be a better Hindu. The same should be the aspiration of all religionists—especially Muslims and Christians. This agrees with what he had learned from Hindus and Jains, that Truth is characterized by "fragmentariness." One needs to learn to respect and live with differences in religious belief and practice.

Gandhi was also a man of action. For him, prayer and meditation were the means of helping those in need. The nearest he got to meditation was repeating the name of God in the Hindi language, *Rr nn an*. This act had for him a mantric power.[5]

The word "God" itself he saw as a stumbling block to interreligious conversation. In his social environment, there were traditions where this concept does not exist, such as Buddhism. Gandhi presented a way out of this impasse. For him, God is Truth. In fact, Gandhi did not have a high regard for theology. Religion was for him a matter of "going about doing good."[6]

These reflections should be sufficient to lead us to an understanding of why Gandhi was so impressed by the Sermon on the Mount. In the next section of this chapter, we will look at an aspect of the Sermon that provides a good contact point for our comparative reflections on Gandhi, Bonhoeffer, and King.

Bonhoeffer's desire to visit Gandhi is tied up with his attraction to the Sermon on the Mount. His work *The Cost of Discipleship* is a treatment of his understanding of the Sermon on the Mount. His approach was mainly based upon a dialogue with Luther's ideas. If he had visited Gandhi, his eyes would have been opened to new insights. But all his attempts to visit India had by that time been aborted.

The East attracted Bonhoeffer's oldest brother, Karl-Friedrich, but his great interest focused upon Russia, its people and political direction. Dietrich, on the other hand, sought an encounter with India. He saw the Indian way of dealing with life as a counterpoint to his own philosophy and theology.[7]

If Bonhoeffer was to take the Barthian distinction between religion and faith seriously, he needed a close-up look at Indian religion and culture. In seeking a plan of action to overcome social injustice, it was not surprising that he was attracted to Gandhi. As Bethge observes, "His natural drive toward action and rational analysis was searching its passive counterpoint of contemplation, intuition, and synthesis. And he was driven by the question of why Christianity had its origin in the East."[8]

Bonhoeffer's desire to meet Gandhi was steadfast. As he became involved in the ecumenical movement in the West, his mind remained trained upon his desired encounter with Gandhi.[9]

As a church theologian, Bonhoeffer was deeply involved in the founding of the Confessing Church. Yet the desire to go to India and get to know Gandhi and his projects persisted.[10] By this time he was becoming disenchanted with Christianity in the West. He observed, "Since I am becoming convinced each day that Christianity is approaching its end in the West, . . . I should like to go to the Far East before returning to Germany."[11]

Bonhoeffer expressed this desire to go to India to some members of his family. He had been in London only three months when the plan to go to India surfaced. Even his involvement in ecumenics and the peace movement did not dissuade him. He received support from his grandmother, Julie, who had encouraged him to take the trip while he was at Tübingen and offered him some financial support. The letter he wrote to her is important. He states, "Sometimes it even seems to me that there is more Christianity in their [Indian] paganism than in our entire Reich Church."[12] He further observes, "Christianity did come from the East originally. But it has been so permeated by civilized thought that, as we can now see, it is almost lost to us."[13]

Karl Barth, as well as other close friends in Berlin and elsewhere, considered Dietrich's obsession to go to India as odd. In a letter to Bonhoeffer in October 1933, Barth made his objections explicit: "Do you remember that business of 'the next ship but one'? And yet the only thing I hear about you in ages is the strange news that you intend to go to India so as to learn some kind of spiritual technique from Gandhi or some other holy man and that you expect great things of its application in the west."[14]

While Bonhoeffer's close friends, such as Hildebrandt, a Jewish-Christian pastor, and Reinhold Niebuhr, were not excited about his Indian plans, he was able to call upon many friends for assistance. Some of his support came from people who knew Gandhi and had participated in his mission. C. F. Andrews, Madeline Slade, Beverly Nichols, and Theodor Lang were among them. Bonhoeffer even underwent tests at the Wellcome Tropical Medicine Institute in London to see if he was physically fit for the tropics.[15]

Bishop Bell of Chichester (Bonhoeffer's ecumenical friend and mentor) wrote a personal letter of introduction for Bonhoeffer to Gandhi. Bell's letter was cordially received by Gandhi, who responded with a friendly letter of invitation. Gandhi invited Bonhoeffer to live with him in his ashram and accompany him on his journeys.[16] Bethge comments that "Bonhoeffer was motivated by the desire to witness Gandhi's exemplification of the Sermon on the Mount—in the spiritual exercises aimed toward a certain goal, and the Indian ways of resistance against tyrannical power."[17]

At this time, Bonhoeffer had a pacifist outlook. He sought a prototype for resistance to Hitler that could induce changes without violence. He had some misgivings concerning the effectiveness of the church struggle, believing that it could become an end in itself by becoming satisfied with confessions and ceaseless activities. He was looking for a means to oppose Hitler that would move beyond the church struggle while remaining legitimate from a Christian standpoint.

Bonhoeffer desired to go to India to absorb the experience and methods of Gandhi before accepting the challenge of directing a seminary for the Confessing Church. Unfortunately, time had closed in on him. The decision now had to be made. He accepted the challenge that awaited him and returned to Germany.[18]

We turn now to King. His appreciation of the Sermon on the Mount and Gandhi's example in living and acting upon its message is direct. We need only provide a brief summary of his outlook here.

King's opposition to the evil of racism was a lifelong project. During his "pilgrimage to nonviolence" in this struggle, he had considered many options. He had studied the insights of Walter Rauschenbush, Karl Marx, William Temple, Reinhold Niebuhr, and others. Even his own encounter with the Western perspectives of the Sermon on the Mount had not provided him with the way to overcome a collective evil like racism in the United States.

A sermon on Gandhi's interpretation of the Sermon on the Mount by Mordecai Johnson, president of Howard University, had a profound impact on King's life, thought, and action. Johnson had just returned from India. King described Johnson's message regarding Gandhi's life, teaching, and mission as "profound and electrifying." As a result, King began a serious study of Gandhi.[19] King observed:

> The whole concept of *satyagraha* (*satya* as truth equals love, and *agraha* is force; *satyagraha* therefore means truth-force or love-force) was profoundly significant to me. As I delved deeper into the philosophy of Gandhi, my skepticism concerning the power of love gradually diminished, and I came to see for the first time its potency in the area of social reform. Prior to reading Gandhi, I had about concluded that the ethics of Jesus were only effective in individual relationship. The "turn the other cheek" philosophy and the "love your enemies" philosophy were only valid, I felt, when individuals were in conflict with other individuals; when racial groups and nations were in conflict, a more realistic approach seemed necessary. But after reading Gandhi, I saw how utterly mistaken I was.[20]

King was impacted by Gandhi and his interpretation of the Sermon on the Mount. He did not meet Gandhi in person, as Bonhoeffer did not. Nevertheless, King was able to translate Gandhi's insights into his understanding of the Sermon and use them in nonviolent direct action. King, however, insisted that Jesus gave him the "message," while Gandhi gave him the "method." King maintained his status as Christian minister-theologian-activist.

Now that we have assessed the deep appreciation Gandhi, Bonhoeffer, and King had for the Sermon on the Mount, we will conclude this chapter by focusing on how each of these religious thinkers understood and applied one statement in the Sermon: "Love your enemies."

GANDHI, BONHOEFFER, AND KING ON "LOVE YOUR ENEMIES"

Upon reading the Sermon on the Mount, Gandhi came upon this passage: "You have heard that it was said, 'You shall love your neighbor and hate your enemy.' But I say to you, Love your enemies and pray for those who persecute you" (Matt. 5:43–44).

Gandhi understood this passage to refer to "nonretaliation" or "nonresistance" to evil. He comments:

> I said to myself, this is what one learns in one's childhood. Surely this is not Christianity. For all I had been given to understand was that to be a Christian was to have a brandy bottle in one hand and beef in the other. The Sermon on the Mount, however, falsified that impression. . . . I saw that the Sermon on the Mount was the whole of Christianity for him who wanted to live a Christian life. It was the Sermon on the Mount which endeared Jesus to me.[21]

Gandhi's attraction to this message in the Sermon did not depend upon accepting a belief in the historical Jesus. He insisted that he would accept the truth of the Sermon even if Jesus had never lived. As far as he was concerned, Christianity was not practiced by so-called Christians. He was certainly put off by the British who professed to be Christian. As long as there is hunger unsatisfied, Christ is not yet born. When real peace is established, we will need no demonstrations.[22]

From this personal testimony of Gandhi's we see that he was looking for truth for his understanding of the moral life. He found what he sought in the Bhagavad Gita and in the Sermon on the Mount. It appears that he would accept Jesus as we in the West would accept Socrates, as a great man with superb moral values, but with no redemptive power. Coming as he did from a territory in India where Jainism was influential, he had knowledge of the concept of *ahimsa* (noninjury), and when he interpreted the Bhagavad Gita, the pan-Indian holy book, in this light, the love ethic of Jesus seemed familiar. For him, the "what" and "how" of the Sermon, rather than the "who," were important. Only if one lived the message in the Sermon did it matter. In his own life, he echoed the comment by Jesus that it is easy to love those who love you. The hard part is to do good to those who mistreat you. It is that which goes beyond what is natural that really counts in religious practice, according to Gandhi.

On a trip from Natal to Johannesburg, South Africa, Gandhi was in a car
on a train that was reserved for white passengers. A white man in the com-
partment attempted to push Gandhi off the train. Somehow Gandhi was able
to hold on to the railing with such strength that the man was unsuccessful.
Other whites made fun of the white man to such an extent that he ceased to
trouble Gandhi. This incident had much to do with Gandhi's experiment in
the use of soul-force in South Africa. This, of course, was the proving ground
for his project in India to overthrow the British Raj.

We turn now to Bonhoeffer, who also was inspired by the same passage in
the Sermon on the Mount. Jesus went beyond the Jewish tradition in his
demand to love one's enemies. Love of enemies is seen as a distinguishing mark
of the followers of Jesus. It is a requirement of Christian "discipleship," which
Bonhoeffer lifts up in his study on this subject.[23]

Bonhoeffer treated the commandment to love one's enemies in *The Cost of
Discipleship*. According to Bonhoeffer, this leads to the meaning of the word
"love." Jesus bids us to encounter our enemies by loving them. Our enemies
are those who are unresponsive to our love, who return nothing when we forgive them. They requite our love with hatred and our service with derision.
True love asks nothing in return, but it seeks those who need love. Bonhoeffer asks, Who needs love more than our enemies, who are consumed with
hatred and who are devoid of love? He reminds us that Jesus tells us how to
behave in relation to our enemies. We are to do good and pray for them.

We are to love our enemies not only in thought and word but also in deed.
We are to be taken along the way to the cross and into fellowship with the Crucified. The more we journey along this path, the surer will be the victory of
our love over the enemy's hatred. Then will we express no longer just our love
but the love of Christ also. We are to remember that Christ went to the cross
for the sake of his enemies.

This self-sacrificing love is a mark that distinguishes the Christian lifestyle.
We find it easy to love those who love us. Nevertheless, the Christian is called
by Christ to do more than what comes naturally. Christians are called to an
extraordinary, unusual, and peculiar kind of loving. This "more," this "beyond-
all-that" is the way of self-renunciation, of an unreserved love for our enemies.
This is a love for the unloved and unloving, for our religious, political, and personal adversaries. This is the love of Jesus Christ, who went to the cross.

According to Bonhoeffer, this type of love has "a hidden nature." The genuine work of love is always hidden, self-forgetful, spontaneous, and unpremed-
itated. Yet it appears ordinary and natural. Because it is hidden, it does not
appear in a visible form or as a visible virtue or habit that one acquires. There
is no calculation of self-interest involved. We look not to ourselves but to the

Christ we are following. By way of emphasis, Bonhoeffer declares, "Thus genuine love spells the end of the 'old Adam' in us, and we recover our true nature in the righteousness of Christ and in our fellow human beings. The love of Christ crucified is the love which lies in those who follow him."[24]

Let us now take a brief look at what Martin Luther King Jr. had to say about the love of enemies. Fortunately, King stated what he sees as essential in this commandment in a sermon with the title, "Loving Your Enemies."[25]

King begins his reflection by pointing out the challenge of this saying. He recalls Nietzsche's observation that this saying indicates that Jesus was "an impractical idealist." Nietzsche observed that the Christian ethic is for weaklings and cowards, for this reason. But King insists, on the contrary, that the love of enemies is not a utopian dream, but a necessity for our survival. We will not be able to solve the problems in our world without practicing this principle. Our responsibility as Christians is to seek an understanding of the meaning of this command and to seek passionately to live it out in our daily lives.

King thus goes forward to suggest three ways to put into practice this summons of Jesus. First, we must develop and maintain the capacity to forgive. Second, we must recognize that the evil actions of the enemy never quite express all that he or she is. An element of goodness is found even in our worst enemy. Third, we seek not to defeat or humiliate the enemy but to win her or his friendship and understanding. We are to remember that reconciliation is our goal. This is, according to King, the practical "how" of the command.

King then turns to the "why" of loving our enemies. First, returning hate for hate multiplies hate. Hate multiplies hate as violence multiplies violence. King observes that this increasing of hate must be stopped or humans will plunge into self-annihilation.

Second, hate scars the soul and distorts the personality. King makes an interesting observation on this point. He connects his experience with that of Bonhoeffer: "We have seen its ugly consequences in the ignominious deaths brought to six million Jews by a hate-obsessed madman named Hitler, in the unspeakable violence inflicted upon Negroes in bloodthirsty mobs, in the dark horrors of war, and in the terrible indignation and injustices perpetrated against millions of God's children by unconscionable oppressors."[26]

Hate is just as injurious to the person who hates as it is to the one hated. King refers to the black social scientist, E. Franklin Frazier, who wrote concerning "the pathology of race prejudice." Frazier had observed normal, amiable, and congenial white persons who were negatively transformed by their hatred of African Americans.

Third, we should love our enemies because love is the only force that can transform an enemy into a friend. Here King lifts up his belief in "redemptive love." He concludes his sermon with this observation: "Love is the most durable power in the world. This creative force, so beautifully exemplified in the life of Christ, is the most potent instrument available in mankind's quest for peace and security."[27]

I can only sum up what King had to say about love here. Reading further into his focus on the love ethic helps us to appreciate more profoundly his teaching and practice about love. We move now into our conclusion, which is a comparison and critique.

CONCLUSION: A COMPARISON AND A CRITIQUE

This chapter is not comprehensive. I have attempted simply to focus upon what these three religous thinkers have in common and on the importance of their lives and activities for the rest of us. Archbishop Desmond Tutu sums up for us what they sensed: "There is no future without forgiveness."

The primary mentors for Bonhoeffer were European, especially Luther and Barth. The primary mentors for King were black Americans (Mays, Kelsey, and Thurman) and personalists at Boston (Brightman and DeWolf). Nevertheless, Bonhoeffer and King admired Gandhi in a passionate manner. Why? What did Gandhi have to offer these theologian-activists? Though he was non-Christian, he had an uncommon influence on both of them.

There is no evidence that either Bonhoeffer or King did serious study in the disciplines of South Asian history and culture or the history and phenomenology of religions. Serious study on the religious, anthropological, and social history of India is essential to appreciate Gandhi in his home context. In addition, his experiences in London and South Africa need to be explored. One would need to be knowledgeable about India's great religions—Hinduism, Buddhism, Islam, and Jainism—as well as the caste system, with its fatalism of the untouchable and the snobbishness and self-righteousness of the Brahman caste.

Unfortunately, Bonhoeffer's association with Karl Barth had given him a confused understanding of non-Christian religions. Barth's robust Christology and limited view of revelation blinded Bonhoeffer to the significance of other religions, with the exception of Judaism. To appreciate Gandhi's method of social transformation, one could not be sidetracked by Barth's veto of non-Christian religions. With a broader view, Bonhoeffer's emphasis on responsibility in the context of time and place would have been severely tested in India. Yet the ecumenical Bonhoeffer who longed for world peace was intensely interested in Gandhi and his nonviolent project.

Bonhoeffer was also disenchanted with Western civilization. His ecumenical work had taken him to several European countries, such as Denmark,

Switzerland, Italy, Spain, England, as well as Eastern Europe. He had more than a "tourist" appreciation of several countries outside Germany. His time in the United States had introduced him to pragmatism, the social gospel, and elements of black culture such as religion, music, and literature. The severity of the race problem had opened his eyes to social injustices.

King was introduced to Gandhi by some of his Morehouse professors. Benjamin Mays, a mentor and a lifelong friend of Daddy King, visited Gandhi. He dialogued with Gandhi and sang Negro spirituals to his delight. Other black religious scholars knew Gandhi personally and observed his movement. Howard Thurman, dean of the chapel at Boston University during King's PhD study there, was one of these. However, it appears that the sermon by President Johnson of Howard University was the linchpin event that sparked King's serious and intellectual consideration of Gandhi's thought and action. He followed this up with research, study, and practice. The Montgomery bus boycott led King to begin using Gandhi's nonviolent technique for social transformation against segregation.

King never met Gandhi in person, although he and Coretta visited India. However, the Kings did not see much of the real India that Gandhi knew. By this time, King had become an international figure and was treated with royal splendor. He was adopted by the upper class and moved mainly in the highest level of society. Still, the Kings saw enough to intensify their struggle against racism at home. In fact, Martin indicated to his wife that he was now poised for a deeper commitment to racial justice at home. What King saw reminded him that Gandhi's work had only started and that the racial struggle in the United States had only been launched.

The legacy of these three martyrs is significant for all who work for humanization in our time. They broke up fallow ground and gave their all to show us the way forward to peace and reconciliation. They did so through a positive understanding of religious ethics in their time and place. Recently we have seen the "dark side" of religious fanaticism. They left behind worthy examples of the power religion can have for good. Paul Lehmann, a close friend of Bonhoeffer, often spoke of religion as a force "to make human life more human." With this assessment I agree.

PART III
Faith and Praxis

10

The Relationship of Church and State in Bonhoeffer and King

Part 3 of this book is an overview of the life, thought, and action of Bonhoeffer and King. The reflection that follows is not merely a looking back at what they said and did in the interest of the liberation of the oppressed. Instead, we will examine their contributions that we might pass on and refine their message and witness for the benefit of this and future generations as they work for the betterment of human relations. Their witness to peace and reconciliation among the peoples of the earth is worthy of serious consideration.

In the decades that have passed since their martyrdom, new initiatives in theological ethics have been expressed in thought and through actions. I have been involved in two: the liberation theology movement and the black church/black theology movement. I was a contemporary of King and a student of Euro-American theologies that informed both Bonhoeffer and King. The perspective I bring here in looking at the witness of these two theologian-activists will bring all of these tributaries of reflection together.

CHURCH AND STATE: THE PROTESTANT TRADITION

Let us begin with a brief look at Bonhoeffer's understanding of the church-state relation. Much of what we say about Bonhoeffer's view could also be applied to King's understanding. Both thinkers were Protestant: Bonhoeffer was Lutheran, and King was Baptist. Nevertheless, both were ecumenical theologians. The difference in their views is largely due to the contexts in which they made their decisions.

Since Bonhoeffer was an ordained minister in the Evangelical Church in Germany, which was both Lutheran and Reformed, we need to have a concise look at both Luther and Calvin on church-state relations. Then the powerful influence of Karl Barth on Bonhoeffer in both thought and action must be taken into account.

Martin Luther's theological distinction between law and gospel could not remain only theological. It led to a need to rethink issues in law, politics, and society. In addition, Luther's protest against canon law in the Catholic tradition left the social order in a moral crisis. This was especially the case in Germany. Thus, the Lutheran Reformation had to broaden itself to include law and issues of statecraft as well. This led to the "two kingdoms" framework for law and theology in the Lutheran Reformation.

According to Luther, God has ordained two kingdoms, or realms, in which humanity is destined to live: the earthly kingdom and the heavenly kingdom. The earthly kingdom is the realm of creation, of natural and civil life, where one operates primarily by reason and law. The heavenly kingdom is the realm of redemption, of spiritual and eternal life, where a person operates primarily by faith and love.

The two kingdoms are parallel. They interact and depend upon each other through biblical revelation and faithful discharge of vocations in the earthly kingdom. But the two kingdoms are ultimately distinct. The earthly kingdom is distorted by sin and governed by law. The heavenly kingdom is renewed by grace and is guided by the gospel. Christians are citizens of both kingdoms and come under the distinctive government of each. As a heavenly citizen, the Christian remains free in his or her conscience, called to live fully in the light of the Word of God. But as an earthly citizen, the Christian is bound by law and called to obey the natural orders and offices that God has ordained for the governance of this earthly kingdom.

In order to appreciate Luther's two-kingdoms doctrine, one needs to observe what he was *against* as well as what he was *for*. For centuries, the medieval church held a traditional hierarchical view of human society. The clergy were called to a higher spiritual service in the realm of grace, the laity to a lower temporal service in the realm of nature. The clergy were exempt from many earthly obligations and foreclosed from many natural activities, such as marriage. Luther turned this hierarchical plan of society on its side. The relation between the two kingdoms became horizontal in Luther's view. Luther's doctrine "laicized" the clergy and "clericized" the laity. He asserted "the priesthood of all believers." He considered the clerical office of preaching and teaching as just one other vocation. Lay Christians could now freely serve God and others.

The traditional ordering of the "two swords," in which the spiritual authority of clerics and canon law was superior to the temporal authority of the magistrate and civil law, was overturned. According to Luther, God has ordained three basic forms of governance of earthly life: the domestic, the ecclesiastical, and the political—or the family, church, and state. All three natural offices were ordained by God at creation. All are equal and all are needed to resist sin in the natural order. But only the state holds the authority of the sword to pass and enforce positive laws for the governance of the earthly kingdom. The church, on the other hand, has no sword and has no law-making authority.

The magistrate is God's vice regent, called to express divine law and reflect divine justice on earth. The magistrate is to be just and fair to all citizens. The ruler is to be as a "father" to the human community over which he rules. Political subjects are to be like children. Citizens are to honor the magistrate as if he were a parent. The duty of the ruler is to protect his subjects in their person and property. The ruler is to deter his subjects from destructive behavior to self and others while he nurtures them in every constructive manner.[1]

We turn now to John Calvin's view on church-state relations. There are similarities in Calvin and Luther on church-state relations. Our modern view of the state as an autonomous entity was foreign to them. Even though both Reformers were in rebellion against the Roman Catholic view of church-state relations, they held thought in the context of the *corpus christianum*. The church and the state were both subject to the sovereign rule of God, the *regnum Dei et Christi*. That is the authority of both spheres inherent in the will and purpose of the living God.

Calvin was mainly concerned with safeguarding the freedom of the church. He was first of all an ecclesiastical statesman, and his interest in the nature and function of the state was secondary. Calvin was interested in the state as a concrete entity rather than a theoretical concern. He approached the state from the viewpoint of the service it can render to the church and to God's kingdom. He differed from Luther on the matter of the state's enforcement of the Ten Commandments. Calvin held that civil government is responsible for enforcing both the first and second tables of the law. Calvin had in his purview opposition in three directions. He opposed the Roman Catholics, who assumed both spiritual and temporal authority; Renaissance theorists, who glorified the secular state; and the Anabaptists, who advocated an anarchistic position regarding the state.[2]

Calvin's position can best be summed up in his own words:

> We believe that God wishes to have the world governed by laws and magistrates, so that some restraint may be put upon its disordered appetites. And as He has established kingdoms, republics, and all sorts of principalities, either hereditary or otherwise, and all that belongs to a just government, and wishes to be considered as their Author, so He has put the sword into the hands of magistrates to suppress crimes against the first as well as the second table of the commandments of God.[3]

BONHOEFFER ON CHURCH-STATE RELATIONS

According to Bonhoeffer, only the concept of government, not the state itself, can have a theological application. Nevertheless, he asserts, a concrete study must involve the concept of state. Likewise, he distinguishes between the spiritual office or ministry and the actual congregation of Christians. The spiritual office is the divinely ordained authority. It does not proceed from the congregation, but from God. He insists that a clear distinction must be drawn between secular and spiritual authority. Christians are, nevertheless, citizens. Citizens, whether believers or not, are subject to the claim of Jesus Christ.[4]

The Reformation did not view the state as arising from the created nature of humans. It placed the origin of the state, as government, in the fall. It was sin that made necessary the divine institution of government. Government is to punish the criminal and safeguard life. Bonhoeffer views the state as rooted in culture. States, according to Bonhoeffer, are divinely permitted political societies. Government, on the other hand, is *ordained* by God. People, culture, social organization, and the like are of the world. Government is order in the world that bears the authority of God. There is, therefore, no Christian state, and the state possesses its character as government independently of the Christian character of the persons who govern.[5] The theological foundation for an authentic government is anchored in Jesus Christ as head of the church.[6]

According to Bonhoeffer, government stands in a certain sense beyond good and evil. It possesses not only an office but also a historical existence. An ethical failure does not deprive it of its divine dignity. He compares government to a relationship between father and son. There can be no ethical isolation of the son from his father. One assumes the guilt of a father or brother. The clearest expression of the dignity of government is its power, the sword that it wields. Even when the government incurs guilt and is open to ethical attack, its power is from God. It has its existence solely in Jesus Christ, and through the cross of Christ it is reconciled with God.[7]

Bonhoeffer goes on to discuss the claim of the government upon the church. The church is to express obedience and respect for government. In the same spirit, there is a claim of the church upon government. The church has the task of summoning the whole world to submit to the dominion of Jesus Christ. In this manner there are ecclesiastical responsibilities of government. Government should protect the righteous and support the practice of religion. In the same spirit, the church has political responsibility. The church has the responsibility to identify sin and injustices in government. The intention of the church's message is to proclaim reconciliation and lift up the grace of Jesus Christ. Individual Christians have political responsibility in the context of the public witness of the church.

Bonhoeffer goes on to suggest certain guidelines for the church-state relationship. He does not choose one form of government, but speaks of the "marks" of the best form of government in relation to the church. First, the best government is one in which the divine origin of government is most evident. Such a government will be from above, from God. Second, the best government sees its power not as endangered but sustained by the maintenance of outward justice, by right of family and labor with a foundation in God, and by the freedom to proclaim the gospel of Jesus Christ. Finally, the best government does not restrict the divine authority conferred upon it, but relates to its subjects in mutual confidence by just action and truthful speech.[8]

Bonhoeffer sums up his view of church-state relations as follows:

> Government and church are bound by the same Lord and are bound together. In their task government and church are separate, but government and church have the same field of action, man [i.e., humans]. No single one of these relationships must be isolated so as to provide the basis for a particular constitutional form. . . . The true aim is to provide room within every given form for the relationship which . . . is instituted by God and to entrust the further development to the Lord of both government and church.[9]

KING ON CHURCH-STATE RELATIONS

King began a serious intellectual quest for a method to eliminate social evil when he entered Crozer Theological Seminary. Part of that quest was an exploration of the relation of churches to the state. This included both the legal and political aspects of statecraft.

For King, government was necessary for a wholesome social life, since humans have the potential for going beyond personal needs in order to gain self-security. He asserted that the force of human sin is so stubborn that a social unit is needed to restrain this tendency. Such a unit must be armed with moral and physical might to curb this tendency. King's view on the nature and action of the state is not easy to describe. It brings together biblical piety, theological liberalism, political advocacy, and social action.

King saw that conservative Christians, black as well as white, were satisfied with the status quo in a segregated society. King challenged all those who believed that religion and politics should seek to sustain things as they are. He must have been confronted often with the advice that Paul gives in Romans 13:1–7. In this biblical passage, Paul urges Christians to obey government authorities with the assertion that the governing authorities "have been instituted by God." King suggested that Paul's message was time and culture bound.

He observed that Christians at that time and place were not concerned with changing the social order, but were looking forward to the "new age" or the "second coming." Segregated America was facing a different order, however, and needed a theological emphasis appropriate for its own situation.[10]

King argued that his thought and action had biblical foundations. He viewed his position as being in the Jesus tradition. King saw his mission as pursuing the kingdom of God on earth. He would not accept the power and jurisdiction of civil authority uncritically.[11] Samuel S. Hill observes that King founded the Southern Christian Leadership Conference (SCLC) in 1957 as a religious-political movement to oppose injustices in government and society at large. King was attempting, according to Hill, to embody the teachings of Jesus in an organization that would change American society.[12]

King believed in strong and aggressive leadership by governmental authorities to sponsor civil rights and social justice. However, when government is on the side of injustice, King believed Christians had the responsibility to apply moral pressure to compel unwilling authorities to yield to the mandates of justice. Government has a responsibility to help control antisocial and immoral behavior through the process of law.[13]

In a passage that ties King with Bonhoeffer, King declares:

> Let us not forget, in the memories of the six million who died, that everything Hitler did in Germany was "legal" . . . In spite of that, I am sure that I would have aided and comforted my Jewish brothers, if I had lived in Germany during Hitler's reign, as some Christian priests and ministers did do, often at the cost of their lives.[14]

For King, the state is fulfilling the divine purpose for its existence when it reflects love and justice, when it creates and preserves the well-being of humans intended by God in Christ. This, in King's judgment, would be a community where integration has replaced segregation, where economic justice has eliminated poverty, and where a just order has supplanted violence and chaos. On the other hand, a state is evil and sinful when it formulates and sponsors policies that are divisive, unjust, and violent.[15]

CONCLUSION

We have now looked at the views of Bonhoeffer and King on the state. It is clear that as theologians they have much in common. Both stand within the Protestant tradition. They see that due to human sinfulness, the state is necessary for positive relations in the human social order. The state has an important role in administering justice, eliminating poverty, and making life wholesome for all citizens.

King is not limited by the restraints from Lutheranism or from Karl Barth that constrain Bonhoeffer. The views of the Boston personalists are evident. The two-kingdoms doctrine of Luther and the veto on natural revelation are not restraints on King's more inclusive christological outlook. Both theologians have a christological understanding of the church-state relation in different contexts.

11

The Context of Decision: Bonhoeffer

BONHOEFFER'S GERMANY: NAZISM AND THE CHURCH STRUGGLE

The brief period between Bonhoeffer's American experience and his encounter with the Nazi regime in some ways is preparatory for the crises to come, from 1933 forward until his death. I have in mind his ecumenical work and his international efforts toward world peace. Ecumenical interests and peace were one in his thinking. Churches united, Bonhoeffer believed, could make a real contribution to world peace. He participated in the activities of the World Alliance of Churches. He believed that if churches could get along together, perhaps nations would also be able to establish peaceful relationships. He had pacifist leanings influenced by his friendship with Jean Lasserre.

Bonhoeffer was only twenty-five years old. He impressed the Alliance with his speech and leadership gifts. He became one of three persons selected at the 1931 Cambridge Conference as an honorary youth secretary. In this position, Bonhoeffer was to coordinate work for the World Alliance in Germany, central and northern Europe, Hungary, and Austria. This involved traveling and planning conferences. Within three years, the German branch of the World Alliance was forced to dissolve. Nevertheless, Bonhoeffer's participation outside of Germany continued. The international contacts he made proved useful later on during the resistance work he was to do.

On September 14, 1930, the Nazis experienced big gains in elections. By the time of the Cambridge meeting of the Alliance in the fall of 1931, Bonhoeffer shared the grim news that many faculty members as well as students at the University of Berlin supported Hitler. Indeed, by the end of 1930, approximately half of the candidates for ordination were followers of Hitler. Bonhoeffer was interested in international relations and peace at a time when Germany was preparing for war. He was encouraged by a goodly number of students at the University of Berlin who supported him. Some of these were to become his students at Finkenwalde.

Bonhoeffer's lectures and talks focused on issues of international cooperation, peace, and the role of the church in the world. In the fall of 1932, Bonhoeffer delivered a talk to the German Student Christian Movement. In this address, he emphasized that God is the God of all peoples and nations, not just Germany. He spoke out against war service. He insisted that every preparation for war is forbidden for the Christian.

During this period of his teaching at the University of Berlin, he lectured and published *Creation and Fall*, based on Genesis 1–3. Since this work was based upon Old Testament texts, scholars were not enthusiastic about his lectures. Nevertheless, some students were impressed.[1]

During this period, Bonhoeffer was ordained, became a student chaplain at a technical college, led a confirmation class, and continued his ecumenical and peace outreach. In the meantime, Nazism was making its impact upon German society. Compared to the bad news in the economy and the political situation, Nazism seemed like good news. Some believed that under the Nazis there would be order rather than chaos. Hitler promised work, which meant food and shelter for hungry families. Many Germans were hungry and unemployed. They resented the fact that in their midst were Jews who were wealthy. These Germans did not notice impoverished Jews or Christians who were prosperous. Hitler took full advantage of such anti-Jewish sentiments. When people heard Hitler speak in the 1930s, they were mesmerized by him. Some looked upon him as if he were a messiah.

Hitler took full advantage of the people's devotion. Leaders in Germany (military, political, and religious) fell under the sway of his promises. Many Christian pastors saw Hitler as a leader who would support the return of strong moral principles. Nazis actually encouraged church attendance and there was considerable church growth under their rule. Hitler promised to turn the unruly youth into a disciplined citizenry. He proceeded to establish the Hitler Youth program to the end that German youth would think and act "German." Of course, Hitler's goal, so obvious later, was to create not a free people but an army that would serve him without question.

Hitler reached down to embrace not only youth but also children. He compared himself to Christ and assured them that like Christ, he would serve their interests. Church leaders encouraged children to accept this personal assessment of Hitler.[2] A popular song taught in the *Jungvolk*, a German boys' organization, illustrates Hitler's approach to young children. The song included these words:

Adolf Hitler is our Saviour, our hero.
He is the noblest being in the whole wide world.
For Hitler we live,
For Hitler we die.
Our Hitler is our Lord
Who rules a brave new world.[3]

It is significant that Dietrich and the Bonhoeffer family were among the first Germans to recognize the dangers of Nazism. In the midst of the capitulation on the part of the German intelligentsia, the Bonhoeffers (Dietrich's parents, brothers, sisters, and his grandmother, Julie) opposed Hitler's plan to take over the German nation for his demonic intentions.[4]

ARYAN CLAUSES AND THE JEWISH QUESTION

Hitler rose to power on a wave of anti-Semitism. Before his "final solution" was put into effect, he legalized a series of discriminatory practices and policies. The most important of these were contained in the Aryan clauses. These clauses disqualified those of Jewish origin, regardless of religious affiliation, from holding office in the state. This disqualification was expanded to include those married to Jews. These measures in the end also imposed the same disqualification on those seeking church appointments. Due to the belief among the "German Christians" that the German church should be truly German, they accepted the Aryan clauses enthusiastically. Bonhoeffer, together with the members of the Confessing Church, refused to accept these laws.[5]

Bonhoeffer's response to this crisis situation seems like double-talk. On the one hand, the church has to accept the state and its laws as they are. The state has its own divine sanction. The church has no clear right or jurisdiction in the activities of the state. The church of Christ, which lives solely from the gospel, cannot expect direct political action. Even considering the "Jewish question," it cannot address the state directly and demand of it some definite action of a different nature. However, the church does not hold an attitude of disinterest. It must continually ask the state if its actions can be justified as legitimate. It can ask if a law or action leads to law and order, or to lawlessness and disorder. This is especially necessary when the state intends to use force in its legal enactments. Consider Bonhoeffer's own statement:

> As long as the state continues to create law and order by its acts, even if it be a new law and new order, the church of the Creator, the Mediator and Redeemer cannot engage in direct political action against it. It may not of course prevent the individual Christian, who knows himself called to the task, from calling the state "inhuman" on occasion,

but *qua* church it will only ask whether the state is bringing about law and order or not.[6]

Bonhoeffer then speaks more forcefully and directly to this matter. He indicates that the state is limited in two respects. Both too much law and order and too little law and order compel the church to speak. He insists that the state that endangers the Christian proclamation negates itself. Furthermore, there are three possible ways in which the church can act toward the state. It can ask the state whether its actions are legitimate and in accordance with its character as state. That is, the church can remind the state of its responsibilities. Then the church can aid victims of state action. In fact, the church has an unconditional obligation to the victims of any ordering of society, even if they do not belong to the Christian community. Finally, there may be instances where more is required than bandaging the victims under "the wheel." The church may find it necessary "to put a spoke in the wheel" itself. This final action on the part of the church may be needed when the state fails to provide law and order or when it brings too much law and order. There would be too little law if any group of citizens were deprived of its human rights, and too much law if the state intervened in the character of the church and its proclamation.

The example Bonhoeffer gives of the state becoming too repressive is directed to the "Jewish question" as follows: ". . . in the forced exclusion of baptized Jews from our Christian congregations or the prohibition of our mission to the Jews. Here the Christian church would find itself in *status confessionis* and here the state would be in the act of negating itself. A state which includes within itself a terrorized church has lost its most faithful servant."[7]

Even in this extreme case, the outlook is paradoxical. When the church is forced to take such action against the state, it is expressing its ultimate recognition of the state. In such case, the church itself is called to protect the state *qua* state from itself and to preserve it. He goes on to say that the "Jewish question" calls for direct political action by the church. However, the action and its form should be decided by an "evangelical council."[8]

At the Barmen Confessional Synod, the false doctrines of the German Christians were declared to be incongruous with the church of Christ. At Dahlem, the Confessing Church set up its own church government and declared itself to be the true church of Christ in Germany.

Because the German church struggle was carried out under the guise of an inner cleavage between the Confessing Church and the German Christians, instead of a clear-cut church-state conflict, the question of fellowship between the two groups became very important. Bonhoeffer addressed this problem. He asserted that the true church can never draw its own boundary, for God alone knows the real members of his church. To attempt to do this would mean to interpret God's call to salvation in a legalistic way. The boundary of the church becomes obvious when it encounters unbelief from the outside and is forced to make a living decision in an objective situation.[9]

A good example of the message and support for the view of the German Christians is found in Emanuel Hirsch, a church history professor, who also taught systematic theology and New Testament at Göttingen University. Hirsch advocated Hitler's election. He and Paul Althaus referred to Hitler's political triumph as "a gift from God." Hirsch joined the Nazi party and became a supporting member of the SS (protective forces). He was, at the same time, dean of his theological faculty. In his academic role, he supported National Socialism in hiring and in curriculum policies. He openly denounced colleagues and students who were not on board with his views.

Hirsch grew up with the so-called Lutheran Renaissance, led by Karl Holl. He shared a pessimistic view of Germany's defeat in World War I and saw Hitler as the great hope for Germany's recovery and future renewal. Hirsch believed in a "God of history" who speaks anew to every generation. In view of his nation's defeat and humiliation in World War I and the Versailles Treaty, when he, Althaus, and others in his circle saw the situation and the promise of relief through Hitler's project, they set out to "save" Germany. They embraced the Nazi position regarding the "Jewish question." Jews, they asserted, could not be part of the rebuilding process. The true German *Volk* was Aryan. Jews were a problem not only in the state but also in the church. Henceforth, according to Hirsch, Jews did not belong in the Christian community. Christians of Jewish descent should be denied a role in the Christian ministry. They were foreigners by race and history. It was proper for a *Volk* church to apply racial criteria to the clergy roster and to insist that only members of the *Volk* should serve.

Hirsch developed his own version of a *Volk* theology. He went so far as to insist that Jesus was not really Jewish but Aryan. He appealed to German critical scholarship on the Bible to establish his views. He no longer accepted the Old Testament as a valuable biblical document. He believed that the contribution of historical-critical analysis on the one hand, and law versus gospel theology on the other, had revealed Judaism to be only a negative counterpoint to the truths of Christianity.

This interlude on the views of Hirsch illustrates the extent to which the leadership among German Christians went to reinterpret Scripture and theology in support of the ideology and project of Hitler and the Nazis.

In a situation in which outstanding scholars and powerful church leaders had taken the position of the Nazis, Bonhoeffer and colleagues had a real challenge. The task for Bonhoeffer was to consider the concrete struggle of the Confessing Church against the German Christians. The Barmen Confessional

Synod declared the doctrine of the German Christians to be false at several points. The Dahlem Confessional Synod asserted that the government of the Reich Church had by its doctrine and actions excluded itself from the true church of Christ. At the same time, the Confessing Church had established its own administrative body and declared itself as the only true church of Christ in Germany. But, Bonhoeffer asks, what does this mean? First of all, its living decisions are to be looked upon as the will of God. Conversely, the Reich Church is at an end. Furthermore, the Lutheran and Reformed churches have joined together as equals. Thus, the Confessing Church has gone beyond the Augsburg Confession—the confession is an ecumenical triumph. Finally, the decisions of the Confessing Church signify an affirmation of Cyprian's famous dictum: *Extra ecclesiam nulla salus*, or "Outside the church there is no salvation." The limits of the church, Bonhoeffer asserts, are the limits of salvation. Thus, anyone who knowingly separates himself from the Confessing Church in Germany separates himself from salvation! This is an existential confession of faith of the true church, Bonhoeffer believed.

In 1942, Bonhoeffer outlined what he believed would provide a conclusion to the church struggle. It called for a lifting of all oppressive measures taken by the state against the German Evangelical Church and a restoration of its complete independence. He called for a new ordering of this body under the leadership of the Confessing Church. He also concluded that the leadership for this church should come from pastors and laity of the young generation who had been tested and proved in the church struggle.[10]

Bonhoeffer's involvement in the resistance movement prohibited his further leadership in the church struggle. His influence in this struggle remained in an unofficial and indirect manner. As Godsey observed: "Someone had to risk throwing himself into the spokes of an insanely driven 'wheel of state,' not only for the sake of the church, but for all the people of a war-torn world."[11]

STATUS CONFESSIONIS

Dietrich Bonhoeffer introduced the concept of *status confessionis* into theological history. Thus, we view this term in the context of his experience in Nazi Germany. It has likewise been used, however, in reference to the witness of the church in South Africa and its *kairos* debate over apartheid in the 1980s. The issues raised by a *status confessionis* have to do with assessing the identity and integrity of the church.

Bonhoeffer shaped the term to denote a situation in which the identity and integrity of the church are being undermined and the gospel is being falsified. Whereas the term *status confessionis* suggests confession and teaching in the church, the modern applications have their context in socio-political and ethical questions. Bonhoeffer suggested seeking a resolution in terms of ecclesiology. For him, *status confessionis* points to a crisis in the church in which the church may cease to be if the crisis is not resolved. The response has more than self-interest in view. The response is a matter of faithfulness and obedience on the part of the church. It has to do with solidarity with the body of Christ, with all its members. The response requires a redefinition of the church's confession and perhaps a regrouping, not as a mere organization but as the body of Christ and as followers of Jesus. Finally, this is to be a reflection upon the nature and praxis of the church in response to a specific challenge.[12] Martin Walton observes: "Crucial to the interpretation of the *status confessionis* is an understanding (confession) of the church as a catholic, that is, an inclusive, human, and therefore ethical community (expressed in fellowship of the reconciled around the communion table of Jesus Christ)."[13]

In Germany on April 1, 1933, Jewish businesses were boycotted and Jews were subjected to violence. On April 7, a "law for the restoration of the professional civil service," also designated as the "Aryan clause," was introduced. This law was directed primarily against Jewish civil servants. There followed the demand to introduce this Aryan paragraph in the German Evangelical Church. This occurred at a rally of the German Christians on April 3–4, even before the civil law was instigated. Another demand was that the church be nationalized with a bishop. Thus, political events became intrachurch affairs.

The central issues for the German Christians were forced acceptance of the Nazi doctrines, including racial purity. The Aryan clause was introduced into churches in the fall of 1933. This led to a protest by Martin Niemöller on November 2, 1933. Niemöller spoke out on behalf of "converted" Jews. However, Niemöller expected Jewish Christians to avoid offense by voluntarily abstaining from positions of leadership. In the meantime, he had established the Pastor's Emergency Union. Members of this body were expected to support his position that the introduction of the Aryan paragraph in the church was a violation of the confession they affirmed. Members of the Pastor's Union were to pledge responsibility for the persecuted, that is, their Jewish Christian colleagues. Thus, the primary concern was for converted Jews. The status of Jews in general was not a live issue.[14]

In this context, Karl Barth produced an essay titled "Theological Existence Today." Barth indicated that he wished to speak "to the point" (*zur Sache*) rather than "to the situation" (*zur Lage*). He observed that the task of the theologian was to practice theology. The church might cease to be the church by not attending to its own subject matter, the Word of God.

Barth asserted that those who belong to the church are members of a community that is not determined by race or blood but by the Holy Spirit and by baptism. It follows that if the German Evangelical Church should exclude Jewish Christians or treat them as second-class Christians, it would cease to be a Christian church. Here again the status of non-Christian Jews was not addressed.[15]

Bonhoeffer wrote Barth in reference to the Aryan issue. He asked Barth what the consequences would be for church membership, unity, and policies. Barth was of the opinion that the *status confessionis* had arrived, even if church leadership only was involved and not membership in general. Barth urged Bonhoeffer to sound the protest. Barth advised continued protest and "a quiet, active, polemic waiting." He suggested that if a schism were to come, to let it come from the other side. Bonhoeffer and his Jewish colleague Franz Hildebrandt were disappointed, and let Barth know of their displeasure. In brief, Barth's position was that a schism must not be forced by self-willfulness or by violence. One must continue to make one's point until expelled. Hildebrandt, a Jewish Christian minister, was impatient with Barth's view.

The Theological Declaration of Barmen of May 1934 was authored by Barth. This was a courageous act of confession on issues facing the German church. It confronted the intervention of the state in church affairs and the threat resulting from splits in the church. It asserted Christ alone (*solus Christus*) as the source of authority and proclamation in the church in the face of those who attributed religious significance to the rise of Hitler and the German nation. Nevertheless, there is no mention of the Jewish question and no reference to the Aryan paragraph.

As a matter of fairness to Barth's position, reference should be made to some of his later statements. In a lecture in December 1938, he spoke out against the persecution of Jews. He even asserted that one who is an enemy of the Jews is an enemy of Jesus Christ. He went on to assert that anti-Semitism is a sin against the Holy Spirit. Anti-Semitism, he remarked, means rejection of the grace of God. Barth skillfully asserted an indebtedness and solidarity with Jews without giving up his emphasis upon Jesus Christ alone.

In a 1967 letter to Eberhard Bethge, Bonhoeffer's biographer, Barth issued a confession of guilt for his lack of concern for Jews in general. He indicated that Bonhoeffer was the first and almost the only one to focus so centrally and energetically on the Jewish question in 1933. He expressed his regret that he omitted this issue in the Theological Declaration of Barmen of 1934. He mentioned that at that time, such a message would not have been well-received in the Confessing Church. He admitted that such possible rejection did not excuse him for this lack in his statements. His mainly "theological" perspective did not target the Jewish question. He was primarily concerned with the place of the Word of God in the church.[16]

Against what we have thus far reviewed in the German church struggle, Bonhoeffer's witness stands out in bright relief. He engaged the Aryan paragraph, with its total Jewish question, head on.

As early as April 1933, Bonhoeffer responded to the Jewish question in an essay titled "The Church and the Jewish Question." Bonhoeffer indicated interest not only concerning baptized Jews in the church but also the church's response to the doings of government. Both issues, according to Bonhoeffer, proved a *status confessionis* for the church. In both instances, the existence, identity, and integrity of church and state were at stake.

Bonhoeffer framed the issue in terms of the Lutheran teaching on the two realms of church and state. The state has its own responsibility to regulate the Jewish question. On the one hand, the church is not to meddle with the affairs of state but, on the other hand, it should inquire into the legitimacy of the actions of government, especially regarding the Jewish question. The church is compelled to speak both in reference to too much law and order as well as too little law and order. There is a lack of law and order when groups of people are deprived of justice and protection. There is an excess of law and order when government interferes in church affairs. In both instances the state negates itself.[17]

In the fall of 1933, Bonhoeffer worked with several others on the Bethel Confession. Although the final text with alterations did not meet with his approval, nevertheless, alongside some unfortunate statements on the disinheritance of Israel by the church is found mention of God's faithfulness to Israel. Bonhoeffer, in his theological reflections on the relationship of the church to Jews, became more interested in the Old Testament. He distanced himself from the ideas of a curse resting upon the Jews, of mission to the Jews, and that the church had replaced and disinherited Israel. Bonhoeffer turned his attention to a critique of the church as he sought a bond with the Jews. As a lone prophet seeking social justice through solidarity with Jews, Bonhoeffer was later to choose the path of political resistance.[18]

In this chapter we have examined the relationship of Dietrich Bonhoeffer to the Jewish question, the Aryan paragraph, and the German church struggle during the reign of Hitler. Bonhoeffer stood out as one who saw the full impact of the sociopolitical oppression of the Jews, especially those who were not baptized. Most of his colleagues limited their concern to Jews who had joined the church. As one who made his views concrete through action, Bonhoeffer now moved into a stage of resistance.[19]

12

The Context of Decision: King

The situation for blacks in the United States needs to be explored in order to understand the time and place of Martin Luther King Jr.'s witness. King himself was aware of the experience of his foremothers and forefathers. The aftermath of slavery was a reality for Daddy King as he grew up in Stockridge, Georgia. The same was true for King's wife, Coretta, as she spent her childhood in rural Alabama. African Americans of King's generation often had kinfolk who could tell their grandchildren about their slavery experience.

THE SHADOW OF SLAVERY

American history is marked by the tragic experience of blacks in slavery, which lasted for hundreds of years. The effects of this blight upon American history cannot be overlooked. It has left its mark on our total society. When any talk of reparations or affirmative action arises, however, many white Americans want to dismiss America's part in this exploitation. After a few decades of affirmative action, they say, "That is enough." But much more time and effort needs to be used to undo the damage done to blacks (and whites) over such a long period. The damage has been intergenerational, and the healing will require much work.

It is interesting to me that liberal Jews in our country, as well as whites, often feel that we should forget slavery and its blight, while they insist that we should remember the Holocaust. They insist that the reason we should not forget that tragic event in modern times is so that it should not happen again. Blacks in the United States, who still see the results of their slave past, live in the hope that this also will not happen again to any people.

Africans were brought over from their homelands to provide free labor in the households and on the plantations of slave owners. Blacks and whites lived in the same spaces and had to negotiate how this close relation would develop. Whites were in control and, therefore, were the ones who decided that the status of blacks would be that of slaves, without economic means or political power. In King's "stride toward freedom" emphasis, we are reminded of our history. He called this "a long night of suffering." The struggle in which he participated continues.

During the long history of our struggle for freedom, we have witnessed many stages and strategies to realize equal rights as persons and citizens of this country. Even the names we have chosen within the last several decades have meaning. We have called ourselves "colored," "Negro," "Afro-American," "black," and "African American." Each one of these terms has had meaning in the context of our struggle to gain freedom, equality, and equal rights in the United States.

The period of the civil rights movement (1954–1970) represents the "Negro" phase of the freedom struggle. This is the period during which King made his powerful witness. Although his personal voice was muted in 1968, his influence has been present through the Southern Christian Leadership Conference (SCLC) and the Martin Luther King Jr. Center in Atlanta. Moreover, the celebrating of his birthday as a national holiday has become an event with ethical, religious, political, and economic meaning. King's witness has continued through the life and witness of those leaders who were personally inspired by him. Andrew Young and Jesse Jackson are outstanding examples.

The climate in race relations in the period 1940–1954 is critical in viewing King's mission. As early as the 1930s, the Supreme Court expressed concern about civil rights, including voting rights, interstate travel, real estate transactions, and other matters. However, it was in the area of public tax-supported education that the Supreme Court would have its primary impact. The National Association for the Advancement of Colored People (NAACP), through its legal unit, took on the bastion of segregation in education in the South.

When the NAACP first tackled inequality in education, many citizens, black and white, believed that upgrading the quality of education in separate locations and facilities would improve the situation. Providing better buildings, equipment, and salaries for teachers and administrators, even changing the title of African American institutions from "college" to "university" were tried by white Southern leaders. All these efforts were ploys used to strengthen Jim Crow.[1]

A team of lawyers educated at Howard University's law school had been preparing a "root and branch" assault on segregation in public schools. Mordecai Johnson, president of Howard, had decided to prepare a group of constitutional attorneys to address the civil rights of blacks in education and other areas of civic and social life.

In 1945, the NAACP held a top-level meeting in New York to address these concerns and change directions. Thurgood Marshall, the NAACP's chief legal representative, stated the organization's new mission: "We decided . . . to make segregation itself our target."[2]

On May 16, 1950, the NAACP filed a suit in the federal court of Charleston, South Carolina, on behalf of sixty-seven African American children, asking that they be admitted to public schools of Clarendon County without regard to race. This case, along with four similar ones, eventually reached the Supreme Court under the name *Brown v. the Board of Education*. In its May 17, 1954, decision, the Supreme Court declared that segregation in public schools on the basis of race is unconstitutional. This reversed the "separate but equal" *Plessy v. Ferguson* decision of 1896. The Court declared that separate educational facilities were inherently unequal and hence deprived the segregated person of equal protection of the laws guaranteed by the Fourteenth Amendment.[3]

The *Brown* decision was soon recognized as a revolutionary step in American race relations. Its implications for education were clear. But, beyond this, it had implications for all publicly operated facilities—libraries, museums, beaches, parks, zoos, golf courses. It covered any field in which segregation was imposed by state law. Although it did not apply to private groups and organizations, it did cause many of them to examine their racial policies.

This decision shook the very foundations of social and legal segregation, especially in the South. The reaction there among many whites was one of shock, anger, and defiant resistance. The White Citizens Council took the lead in resistance among business and professional people. The Ku Klux Klan mobilized the lower-income groups.[4]

In the 1950s, especially with such court decisions, the African American battle for equality moved at a much faster pace. This was a period of personal awakening for me, as a theologian and ordained Baptist minister based at Howard University. Though I had experienced as a southerner many of the worst aspects of racial exploitation and hate, I had not taken the foreground in this struggle.

Observing how my university was participating in the struggle, especially in the courts and in education, I began to be more active in the struggle for freedom and equality. In 1962, I was invited to be a member of a seminar on theology and law at Duke University's divinity school. That university was not yet desegregated. However, a professor of Christian ethics, Waldo Beach, invited me to join his seminar. His courage was very inspiring to me. After this summer seminar, I returned to Howard and entered into conversation with Dean Spottswood Robinson. Robinson had been on Thurgood Marshall's legal team in the *Brown* case. The result of my conversation with Dean Robinson was a religion and law seminar at Howard. The intent of the seminar was to create a dialogue between ministers and lawyers on racial equality and other common concerns.[5]

During my dialogue with black attorneys in the field, I learned that some felt that Martin Luther King Jr.'s activities were antithetical to the legal approach to black freedom. They did not understand King's Christian confessional stance, his method of nonviolent action, or his more philosophical understanding of law. They knew "case law," but many had no appreciation for jurisprudence. King, they believed, was getting in the way of progress being made through the courts. Their critique was very enlightening and helpful for my perspective.

During this period of the civil rights movement, churches were aroused. These were mainly black churches, but some white congregations and even denominations entered the struggle for racial equality. As a theologian and minister based at Howard, I was a participant in the religious dimension of the struggle. An annual Institute of Religion at Howard brought together religious campus leaders, pastors, chaplains, and scholars from across the nation. Some issues of great concern related to black freedom were usually discussed. Literature produced in these sessions was published through the *Journal of Religious Thought*. In this context there developed a strong theological and ethical ferment, which engaged many of us who were just beginning our vocation.

In the meantime, the movement led by King was receiving much attention. On December 1, 1955, the seamstress Rosa Parks boarded a bus in Montgomery, Alabama, and refused to respect the segregated seating laws of the city. She was arrested. The Montgomery Improvement Association, with King as president, was the result.[6]

King's "I Have a Dream" speech must be put in context if its true meaning is to be understood. It followed the bloody campaign in Birmingham after which an agreement was forged between King and his followers and the business community. Before this agreement was reached, however, President John Kennedy, Attorney General Robert Kennedy, and federal troops had to get involved. King had considered Birmingham as a real challenge for nonviolent direct action. Birmingham was the largest industrial city in the South. It had a history of entrenched racism and injustice. The police commissioner, Bull Connor, had sponsored a reign of terror in that city, and Alabama's governor George Wallace had vowed "segregation forever." Thus, King saw Birmingham as "the most segregated city in America."[7]

On April 16, 1963, King wrote his famous letter from a jail cell in Birmingham in response to a summons from white ministers to cease demonstrations in that city. They considered King to be a troublemaker and an "outsider" who was inciting violence in Birmingham.

The year 1963, prior to the March on Washington, was an eventful one, especially if one views the events in Birmingham. Among those events were the brutal treatment of demonstrators by Bull Connor. Dogs and fire hoses were used on a thousand children as well as older marchers placed under arrest. The repression in that city was an embarrassment to a nation that claimed to be a democracy. The Birmingham campaign had exposed the real depths of racism.[8]

President Kennedy announced a new civil rights proposal on June 11, 1963. Mississippi NAACP leader Medgar Evers was assassinated on June 12, 1963, and President Kennedy met with King on June 22, 1963. All these events preceded the March on Washington.

King described this march as the most significant and moving demonstration for freedom and justice in the history of this country.[9] A. Philip Randolph, a seasoned group organizer, led the planning of this march. On August 28, more than two hundred thousand people of all faiths, black and white, people of every condition of life, stood together before the stone memorial of Abraham Lincoln in the nation's capital. King observed: "We had strength because there were so many of us. . . . We had dignity because we knew our cause was just. We had no anger, but we had a passion—a passion for freedom. So we stood there, facing Mr. Lincoln and facing ourselves and our own destiny and facing the future and facing God."[10]

The march was so impressive that, in King's words, "everyone who believed in man's capacity to better himself had a moment of inspiration and confidence in the future of the human race."[11] This was, indeed, a mountain peak experience.

In order to appreciate the complete witness of King to the church and to humanity, one needs to consider his leadership after the March on Washington. It is unfortunate that many Americans of all persuasions in religion and politics view the "I Have a Dream" speech as the peak of King's witness, even more so because this classic address to the nation is generally understood only in regard to the optimistic emphasis in the message. However, King lifted up in this speech the dark side of our nation's racial history. He also referred to the present and the future. Pondering his words throughout the speech, one gets a look at the challenge ahead. The events that followed, between the remainder of the year 1963 and his death in 1968, were more like a "nightmare" than a "dream." King himself viewed this speech as affirming that progress had been made. Nevertheless, obtaining "dignity"—sitting at lunch counters and riding buses and trains on a nonsegregated basis—is not all that is needed. Equality in employment, housing, and so forth was still to be pursued.

SOME NONVIOLENT PROTESTS LED BY KING

Albany, Georgia

In this protest, King attempted to use what he had learned in Montgomery as a means of nonviolent change in Albany. He sought to cooperate with the local black leadership and with the Student Nonviolent Coordinating Committee (SNCC) to transform the relationship between blacks and whites in that city. His goal was not just to integrate facilities and services but to stamp out the rigidly segregated lifestyle there.

There were major differences in the outlook of the groups involved in this effort. This went beyond the differences between the SNCC and the SCLC to include local black and white leaders.

King soon realized that nonviolence based upon theological assertions and ethical perspectives was not an irresistible force to overcome the grip that segregation had over the people in Albany. He met disunity, distrust, and disagreement over strategy and ideology.

The Albany movement was not well planned. The objectives were too general. King did not get the assistance he anticipated from the federal government. Thus, Albany was a sobering experience for King. King learned that any method of social protest and change depends upon many factors if it is to be effective. Albany was in many ways a failure. On the other hand, what King learned there would be useful in future struggles for human rights and social justice.[12]

Birmingham

When King moved into Birmingham, he made sure that the goals were specific. He decided to concentrate on the business community. First, the buying power of blacks was significant. A prior boycott had already caused businesses to lose money. Second, the downtown area was small; therefore, demonstrations could be effective. Third, many merchants had indicated their willingness to negotiate and desegregate if permitted to do so by city officials. Fourth, some stores were part of nationwide companies. Organizers believed that pressure from their northern headquarters could be applied to bring about changes in racial policies. Fifth, organizers expected that merchants who were willing to change could use their influence to persuade other white leaders to talk with black leaders in order to make needed changes. Stores with lunch counters were targeted first. The integration of lunch counters was mainly symbolic; however, it did have the possibility of opening up negotiations.

King had to reflect on how to deal with the Birmingham protest legally. Elsewhere legal injunctions had stalled and occasionally, as in Albany, defeated his efforts to bring about social change. He recalled the assertion by Thoreau that one should refuse to cooperate with unjust laws. But one should also be willing to accept imprisonment, if that is the consequence. He advocated this principle among his followers in Birmingham.[13]

King believed now that a successful protest through mass demonstration should begin slowly but move steadily to a climax. A legal injunction against mass demonstrations, if obeyed, could defeat the effort. King planned carefully and sought to get the black community behind his effort. He began with a token street demonstration on April 6, 1963, the day before Palm Sunday. The police response was mild. An injunction was delivered to King on April 10. Two days later, on Good Friday, King issued a defiance of the injunction. King and his close aides were arrested. The police, under the leadership of Bull Connor, resorted to violence as the demonstrations continued. Support in the community turned to the demonstrators. Responding to an appeal from white Christian and Jewish leaders, King wrote his famous "Letter from a Birmingham Jail." He then posted bond and resumed leadership of the movement.[14]

Watley concludes that King's experiences in the Albany, Birmingham, and Selma campaigns helped to refine his ethic. Of course, Montgomery had laid the foundation. In this first nonviolent effort, the black community had gained pride and self-confidence, which could initiate political and economic change. Albany was in many respects a failure. But even there King had learned much that made his efforts more effective elsewhere. Birmingham had opened up public accommodations for black citizens. Selma turned out to be the most successful protest in that period.[15]

Selma

Selma was especially important in that it engaged a major national issue and sought to influence the executive and legislative branches of the federal government. This breakthrough unearthed the plight of blacks on the economic front. The economic system had so maimed the masses of black folk, North as well as South, that they were unable to take advantage of the doors that were opened in the civil rights struggle up to that point. Thus, economic justice became the next emphasis of King's nonviolent movement. Watley even suggests that the first phase of the movement ended in Selma and that a second phase began there. The second phase would be both national and global.[16] We will examine the leadership of King in this period in chapter 14.

13

Speaking Truth to Power: Bonhoeffer

The next two chapters are the apex of our study. We have been leading up to the way in which Bonhoeffer and King each expressed his passion for social justice. We have been seeking an understanding of the manner in which these two activist-theologians discerned "the divine presence" as they confronted "human power."[1]

As we face a world filled with terror and unrestrained violence, these church theologians indicate that there is a positive side to religious involvement in power politics. Their life witness is beneficial to us as we seek to enhance the quality of life for countless humans in the global community today. They offered their lives on behalf of those who were victimized by poverty, power-lessness, and many forms of oppression. They restored our confidence in the redeeming and healing essence of faith in action.[2]

There is in many circles a belief that social change can best be accomplished by those who have renounced faith in a Supreme Being, who assert that humans are on their own in an evil-infested world. They believe that we humans provide the best hope for the transformation of society for the common good.

Bonhoeffer and King represent examples of theologians of the Christian faith who, as ministers and scholars, interpreted the faith as a powerful force for social justice. They demonstrated compassion and the humane use of power. We will now consider in turn the contribution that our theologians made to our theme, "Speaking Truth to Power."

RADICAL CHRISTOLOGY
AND POLITICAL RESISTANCE

Here we are interested in how Bonhoeffer's perspective regarding power politics moved from a rigid pacifism to political resistance. The final stages of his decision making and activism led to the sacrifice of his life for others. My reflections will survey this "witness unto death" for the oppressed.

It is important to study Bonhoeffer's thought and life to comprehend this final phase of his unusual testimony. His early theological reflection in *The Communion of Saints* laid a foundation for the rest of his life of action. This is where we must begin.

In this first major study, Bonhoeffer described Christ as "a collective person" and went on to assert that the church is "Christ-existing-as-community." In a word, he brought sociology and theology together as the basis for his lifetime theological outlook.

In his Christology lectures, Bonhoeffer demonstrated how central the person and work of Christ is to his total affirmation of faith. Christ is, indeed, the "center" of his faith claim. He emphasizes the "who" of Christology. For Bonhoeffer, Christ is "with us" in Jesus. It is essential to him that the Word became flesh in our midst.

Bonhoeffer developed a perspective on Christology that places Christ in the center of our world, our history, and our life. Christ is the "one for others" who demonstrates a redeeming compassion for each and every human being.

The historic Jesus, a Jew, was important to Bonhoeffer. But Christ, the God-man, brings heaven and earth together. Bonhoeffer's awareness of the sin and evil inherent in humans led him to take the saviorhood of Jesus Christ seriously. He affirmed the divinity as well as the humanity of Christ. He was concerned with Christology from "the crib" to "the cross" and beyond. However, Bonhoeffer emphasized the cross and the redemptive suffering of Jesus as the Christ on our behalf. Another way of stating the case is that for Bonhoeffer, the Jesus of history is the Christ of faith. As sinful humans, we need more than a moral example; we need a savior. We need the benefits of what Bonhoeffer describes as "costly grace."

This "radical Christology" is the foundation for Bonhoeffer's "ethical" theology, as James Burtness has described it.[3] Burtness asserts that for Bonhoeffer, "theology is rationally prior to ethics. Theology is the noun, ethics the adjective. It is the Man for others who leads his followers to be for others. The problem of Christian ethics is the realization among God's creatures of the revelational reality of God in Christ."[4] Benjamin Reist has also observed that Bonhoeffer is doing ethical theology. This type of theology "concentrates on the pressure on today of the imminent tomorrows—not the distant tomorrows—but the ones close in, in which the God who is real in Jesus Christ is imminent."[5]

Burtness sees the radical nature of Bonhoeffer's ethics as based upon the focus on the person of Jesus Christ, rather than reflections or speculations about him. This outlook is constant in Bonhoeffer's life and thought. Bonhoeffer makes this plain himself:

There is earnestness only in the reality of God and the reality of man which became one in Jesus Christ. . . . There is no Christianity in itself, for this would destroy the world; there is no man in himself, for this would exclude God. . . . Only the God-man, Jesus Christ, is real, and only through Him will the world be preserved until it is ripe for its end.[6]

THE CONTEXTUAL DECISION

Gaining a working knowledge of Bonhoeffer's ethical outlook is not easy due to the fact that his life was cut off before he completed his *Ethics*. Our concern here must simply be determining how he made crucial decisions. He made certain representative statements: "proving the will of God," "conformation," the "ultimate" and the "penultimate," "the command of God" and the question, "What is the meaning of Christ for us today?" These are clues to his manner of making decisions. I have studied several specialists, but have decided to follow the direction that Larry Rasmussen has pursued. He has settled with two foci, "ethics of formation" and "ethics of command," which he attempts to bring together as he concludes his exploration of the method of decision making in Bonhoeffer.[7]

Let us look first at ethics of formation. In this perspective we encounter what Bonhoeffer describes as "mandates." Mandates are aspects of the human situation. Family and state are representative of the natural characteristics of human social and cultural existence. Mandates are the media of conformation.

In *The Communion of Saints*, Bonhoeffer seeks to explore the social character of revelation. He discusses the incarnate God as existing "in, with, and under" social relations. In *Act and Being*, we encounter the concrete g*estalt Christi*—Christ in the form of the ecclesial community. Bonhoeffer is quite explicit when he says, "God is not free *of* man but *for* man. Christ is the Word of his freedom. God is there . . . not in eternal non-objectivity but . . . is 'havable,' graspable in his Word within the Church."[8] Bonhoeffer clearly rejects any basis for Christian moral judgment outside of Christ.[9]

There is a progression in Bonhoeffer's ethics of formation as a means to make decisions. The contextualization perspective in ethics moves toward universal rights, duties, and relationships. These may vary through time and be imbedded in cultures and history. But they share the coherence and continuity of Christ's own form in the world. Bonhoeffer even speaks of "natural piety" and of "unconscious Christianity."

We now move on to ethics as command. As early as the Barcelona lectures, Bonhoeffer used language descriptive of a command. For instance, he speaks of "being addressed," "God's call," and "claim." Note the following statement:

> Thus there cannot be ethics in a vacuum, as a principle; there cannot
> be good and evil as general ideas, but only as qualities of will making
> a decision. These can be only good and evil as done in freedom. . . .
> Bound up in the concrete situation, through God and in God the
> Christian acts in the power of a man who has become free. He is under
> no judgment but his own and that of God.[10]

Bonhoeffer emphasizes that a command should be definite, clear, and
timely. It should be based upon reference to concrete realities and places. The
command is a specific, prophetic word to a concrete situation, or it is not God's
command.[11] Thus, Bonhoeffer insists that "the commandment of God is permission. It differs from all human laws in that it commands freedom."[12]

Bonhoeffer states his position in these words:

> God's commandment is always concrete speech to somebody. It is
> never abstract. . . . It is always an address, a claim, and it is so com-
> prehensive and at the same time so definite that it leaves no freedom
> for interpretation or application, but only the freedom to obey or dis-
> obey. . . . The commandment of God becomes the element in which
> one lives without always being conscious of it, and thus it implies free-
> dom of movement and action, freedom from the fear of decision, free-
> dom from fear to act; it implies certainty, quietude, confidence,
> balance and peace.[13]

Rasmussen attempts to bring the method of formation and the method of
command together in a convenient summary. Both stress concreteness, con-
textuality, and relationality, and they are located in a fixed time and place. The
mandates play an indispensable role in each method. Both methods point to
moral action. Obedience to the command of God is for moral content. This
is identical with conformation in Christ.

In both methods the direction is from the question and answer about the
indicative to the question and answer about the imperative: from "How is
Christ taking form among us here and now?" to "What action on my part con-
forms to his action?"; from "What is God-in-Christ commanding here and
now?" to "What action on my part is in keeping with this command?" The
stress is on the indicative. It is permissive and authorizing.[14]

Deputyship or vicarious action is expressed in both methods. The supreme
ethical deed is the deed of free responsibility. Such an act is an expression of
reality at a particular time and place. The final judgment of the deed lies in the
hands of God. Both approaches to ethical decision are grounded in justification by grace.[15] Since Bonhoeffer's statement is unfinished and incomplete, the
two perspectives arrive at a point of convergence. Bonhoeffer's approach to
ethical decision is contextual in a comprehensive sense.

PACIFISM, POLITICAL RESISTANCE, CONSPIRACY, AND MARTYRDOM

As we move toward a consideration of the decision that ended Bonhoeffer's witness and life, there are several key matters to consider. Bonhoeffer's stress upon concreteness, reality, responsibility, freedom, and the time and place for decision is useful to our reflection. In addition, Bonhoeffer was ecumenical in experience and thought. His concern for the unity of the churches was important to his outlook. He had a passion for fellowship in small and large assemblies of Christians. He was committed to understanding the church theologically as a community, indeed, as the body of Christ. Finally, as he looked closely at the world situation, especially the crisis in his beloved homeland, he invested much effort in seeking world peace. However, he found himself advocating peace as his country prepared for war.

In the early 1930s, Bonhoeffer was preoccupied with the Christian witness for peace. This was related to his work with the World Alliance of Churches. This organization represented liberal idealistic internationalism. It was founded on the eve of the war of 1914 through the development of European and American peace advocates. Bonhoeffer was concerned that the World Alliance lacked theological undergirding. It operated with pragmatism and rationality. Due to its important mission, Bonhoeffer threw himself energetically into its activities.

There was a problem concerning the ecclesial status of the World Alliance. Its membership was made up of enthusiasts for world peace rather than serious representatives of the churches. Fortunately, a parallel body emerged in 1925, the Universal Christian Council for Life and Work. The latter body was in the mainstream of the ecumenical movement. The two bodies overlapped and entered into a cooperative relationship. The high point came at a conference held in Fanø, Denmark, in 1934.

A friendship developed between Bonhoeffer and the Anglican bishop of Chichester, G. K. A. Bell, who was chair of the Council for Life and Work. A personal friendship across lines of confession and nationality was an important aspect of the ecumenical movement. This friendship between Bonhoeffer and Bell was especially important during the Second World War. At Fanø, Bonhoeffer was invited to membership in the Council. The Alliance crumbled under the Nazi state, and in Germany the Council for Life and Work took on the witness for peace.

At the Confessing Church's seminary in Finkenwalde, Bonhoeffer included the peace witness in his teaching. From his pacifist position, Bonhoeffer insisted that the refusal to embrace military service should include his students, even Lutherans.

At Fanø Bonhoeffer made his most powerful statement on behalf of peace and nonviolence. His premise was that peace is not first a human wish to be arrived at by human technique and effort. Peace lies in God's own reconciling work in Christ, of which the church is a sign and witness.[16] He issued a call for a universal council of all churches to reject war and to declare peace as God's will and promise to the whole world:

> Only the one great Ecumenical Council of the holy church of Christ over all the world can speak out so that the world . . . will hear, so that the peoples will rejoice because the church of Christ in the name of Christ has taken the weapons from the hands of their sons, forbidden war, proclaimed the peace of Christ against a raging world.[17]

POLITICAL RESISTANCE

In spite of Bonhoeffer's attraction to Gandhi and the way of nonviolence, as well as his own commitment to pacifism and sympathy for conscientious objectors, Bonhoeffer entered into a stance of resistance against the state.

Bonhoeffer was a patriot. He loved his country and its people. Yet he had become deeply convicted about the virtual unredeemability of the national order in his home country. He knew of horrors that impelled action. He had knowledge of German war crimes. In spite of his Lutheran background with its two-kingdom doctrine, this was for him the exception that had to be addressed.

According to Bonhoeffer, there are certain criteria one must consider in relation to a political resistance stance. First, there must be clear evidence of gross misrule. Bonhoeffer was opposed to totalitarian rule. He insisted upon the rule of law, believed in a distribution of powers, and promoted the guarantee of certain rights. He was not opposed to all forms of strong government. He was not an unqualified democrat. He affirmed a morally responsible Prussian conservatism.

Second, Bonhoeffer asserted that the scale of political responsibility must be respected. A class structure was in his purview. Persons of lower ranks in the social hierarchy were not to take on heavy political responsibility unless those of higher rank abdicated their responsibility.[18] Bonhoeffer states his view as follows: "According to Holy Scripture, there is no right to revolution, but there is responsibility of every individual for preserving the purity of his office and mission in the *polis*."[19]

Third, coercion must be the last resort. All nonviolent and legal means must first be exhausted or known in advance to be clearly unavailing before one considers violent and illegal means. In the final analysis, Bonhoeffer allows the use of violence toward persons, including the possibility of assassination.[20]

Bonhoeffer viewed the Nazi reign of terror as mandating an exception to the normal response to an unjust situation. In the language of Kierkegaard, he advocated a "teleological exception to the ethical" in this instance. The Nazi practice of genocide was the basis for tyrannicide, the assassination approach to terminate the reign of Hitler. The Third Reich had forfeited its legitimacy as a state. There was, therefore, the necessity to restore the rule of law by extraordinary means. Bonhoeffer even suggested that the opposition to Nazi rule might include the employment of some of the tactics used by the Nazis: deception, force, and violence. But the ends and disposition would be anti-Nazi. The goal would be the return of justice via law, against the rule of barbarity via laws and orders that were arbitrarily formulated and enforced. Rasmussen's observations are supported by Eberhard Bethge in these words:

> The one who uses exceptional violence will acknowledge the guilt he or she incurs in its use, and will seek forgiveness. When violence is the last of the last resorts, when the extraordinary exception is never allowed to become standard policy, and when the ends and dispositions are themselves just, then the extremes of active resistance might be turned to in order to topple an order that cannot be healed from within.[21]

THE CONSPIRACY

With a conviction that the situation required putting "a spoke in the wheel" of the state, Bonhoeffer decided to speak for the speechless and act for the powerless. The Confessing Church was not sufficiently outspoken in view of the extreme situation of injustice. Even the Barmen Declaration did not address forcefully the Jewish question. Its emphasis upon *solus Christus*, Christ alone, was inadequate. The reality was that there was a tendency to abstain from political participation in the face of increasing injustice.

The official Reich Church decreed, as a birthday gift for Hitler after the invasion of Austria, that all pastors should take an oath of allegiance to Hitler personally. Many Confessing Church pastors accepted this challenge, and even the Confessing Synod complied.

The legal decrees during this period (1938 forward) involved Bonhoeffer in a personal way. His brother-in-law, Hans von Dohnanyi, was able to keep the Bonhoeffer family abreast of Nazi intentions. There were passport designations on all non-Aryans, and the new military call-up included persons of Bonhoeffer's age. The so-called "Crystal Night" of November 9, 1938, was very destructive toward Jewish people and institutions.

Bonhoeffer's twin sister, who was married to a Jewish man, took flight to England with her family. In 1939, Dietrich was invited by Reinhold Niebuhr and

Paul Lehmann to return to New York. They had arranged work for him. He went to America for a brief period. While there he produced a diary that reveals the agony of his decision to return to his "destiny" in Germany. He decided that his second trip to America in 1939 was a mistake. He concluded that if he did not live through the war years with his people that he would not be useful to them in the period of reconstruction.[22] The essence of his decision is stated in these words: "Christians in Germany will face the terrible alternative of either willing the defeat of their nation in order that Christian civilization may survive, or willing the victory of their nation and thereby destroying our civilization. I know which of these I must choose, but I cannot make this choice in security."[23]

Upon his return to Germany, Bonhoeffer soon became a member of the Abwehr, a German military intelligence agency. This agency was, ironically, the center of German resistance to Hitler. The Gestapo assumed that Bonhoeffer's ecumenical contacts could help in gathering information that would be useful to the war effort. This position enabled Bonhoeffer to travel to Switzerland, where he met Karl Barth, and to Sweden, where he met Bishop Bell, his chief ecumenical contact from London. His real purpose was to help Jews escape from Germany and get support from the Allies for the German resistance. In this role in the resistance, Bonhoeffer was isolated from the church. He found a new community among his secular co-conspirators.[24]

The conspiracy in which Bonhoeffer and Dohnanyi were involved began to come unraveled when Bonhoeffer's phone was tapped in his parents' house. On April 5, 1943, he was arrested. His time in prison allowed for much reflection upon decisions he had made. He made the following observation to Bethge:

> Now I want to assure you that I haven't for a moment regretted coming back in 1939—nor any of the consequences either. I knew quite well what I was doing, and I acted with a clear conscience. . . . And I regard my being kept here as being involved in the fate of Germany in which I was determined to share. I look back on the past without any self-reproach and accept the present in the same spirit.[25]

REFLECTION ON MARTYRDOM

In his foreword to *The Cost of Discipleship*, Bishop Bell writes of Bonhoeffer: "He was crystal clear in his convictions. . . . He saw the truth and spoke it with a complete absence of fear."[26] A further statement sums up Bell's impression of Bonhoeffer as an emissary from the opposition (in 1942): "He was . . . completely candid, completely regardless of personal safety, while deeply moved by the shame of the country he loved."[27]

The witness to truth in the face of the abuse of power was characteristic of Bonhoeffer's life. In February 1933, he had denounced on the radio a political system that would corrupt and mislead a nation and make the "Führer" its idol and god.[28]

Leibholz seeks to explain Bonhoeffer's reflections that led to his "obedience" and in turn to his death. His decision to engage in an act of tyrannicide did not come easily. Nevertheless, he moved away from the traditional Lutheran view, that politics and religion are totally separate, for a good reason. He came to recognize that the political authority in Germany had become entirely corrupt and immoral and that a false faith is capable of terrible and monstrous things. For Bonhoeffer, Hitler was the anti-Christ who enjoyed destruction, slavery, death, and extinction for their own sake. Hitler was the anti-Christ who desired to pose the negative as positive and as creative.

Bonhoeffer was firmly convinced that a Christian has both a right and a duty toward God and humanity to oppose tyranny. Hitler showed total disregard for natural law and the will of God. Any form of totalitarianism that will force humans to cast aside religious and moral obligations to God and subordinate the laws of justice and morality to the state is incompatible with the meaning of life and Christian love. Bonhoeffer had become convinced that, if need be, a Christian must offer his or her life to prevent this from becoming the order of things to come. While he believed that the Confessing Church should cease to be silent and take a stand for what was true and just, he did not commit the church to his actions. He was willing to take upon himself the responsibility of his decision.[29] Bishop Bell begins his foreword to *The Cost of Discipleship* by quoting Bonhoeffer's bold confession that, at the end of Bonhoeffer's life, was fulfilled: "When Christ calls a man, he bids him come and die."[30]

Even if we cannot fully understand or endorse the decision of Bonhoeffer to participate in the attempt to rid his country and the world of Hitler and the Nazi regime, we can appreciate the serious and extraordinary decision that Bonhoeffer made. He was not a self-appointed vigilante, but one of a substantial group of German resistance leaders who decided that Hitler had to be overthrown. It was for Bonhoeffer a choice between two evils. He decided that he would assume the responsibility for this action. He would also accept the guilt. Upon offering up his life for this cause, he would ask for God's forgiveness.[31]

This decision was agonizing and seriously considered. It was consistent with Bonhoeffer's life, thought, and commitment to be for others in their oppression and suffering. It stemmed from his theology of relationship and responsibility and his conviction that he should speak for the voiceless and suffer on behalf of the powerless. For him, the church was "for others" and Christ is the one for others. This decision, as unusual as it may be, was based upon what Bonhoeffer deemed to be concrete reality in its time and place. He therefore observed that his death was "the end and the beginning of life."[32]

14

Speaking Truth to Power: King

We have considered the manner in which Bonhoeffer made decisions and have acknowledged his final decision, which led to his death for the cause he embraced. We will look now at the method King employed in decision making and the manner in which he arrived at the decision that led to his final demise.

At first glance, it would appear that King's thought and action are easily understood. However, this outlook is deceptive once one begins to explore his reflection and the manner in which he actively followed his convictions, with obedience unto death. We will first explore his method of decision making as well as the thinking that undergirded his actions. Then we will look at the way he applied his understanding of the best ethical decision in the final years of his life.[1]

KING'S ETHICAL METHOD

Any real appreciation of King's approach to ethical decision making must begin with a look at his experience of the black family, church, and community. This was the basis for his worldview. Much of King's witness was fueled by his upbringing in the black experience. I would attribute much to his parents and to the Ebenezer Baptist Church in Atlanta. The seedbed of King's early intellectual preparation was Morehouse College. His encounter with leading minister-scholars at Morehouse provided a solid foundation for what he received in intellectual refinement at Crozer and Boston University. Scholars who begin with King's study in the North under predominantly white professors miss an encounter with the real Martin Luther King Jr. Who he *became* is based upon who he *was* in those early years of preparation in the black South.[2]

With this initial reminder of King's roots in the black experience, we can appreciate how he was able to accept as well as reject much that he encountered as he forged his own method for making ethical decisions. In the discussion that follows, I will set some limits. I will focus on how King made ethical decisions, and I will be mainly concerned with his engagement with collective evil.

King described evil as positive and aggressive. Here he went against a tradition in Christian thought that goes back to Augustine. For King, evil is not a form of "privation" of goodness; it is both positive and aggressive.[3] He asserted that evil is a stark and real entity. He recalled the exodus account that describes Pharaoh's resistance to the freedom struggle of the people of Israel: "Evil is recalcitrant and determined and never voluntarily relinquishes its hold short of persistent, almost fanatical resistance."[4] In 1967, he warned, "Evil must be attacked by a counteracting persistence, by the day-to-day assault of the battering rams of justice."[5]

New Testament scholar Carl H. Marbury recalls the Southern and black "fundamentalist" cultural tradition of King. In that tradition, the basic tenets of the Christian tradition are to be believed; they are not to be validated as scientific facts. King did not spend a lot of effort discussing such matters. He reveals a brilliant intellect that was somewhat eclectic. He did not believe that Christianity had a monopoly on truth. He was conversant in many disciplines and with many great minds. He had a special capacity for arriving at a creative synthesis of ideas. This he used in making decisions throughout his short life.[6]

John Ansbro, in his impressive interpretation of King's thought, has referred to a number of thought systems that influenced King. Among these are those of Gandhi, Plato, Anders Nygren, George Davis, Harold DeWolf, Howard Thurman, Kant, Nietzsche, Socrates, Reinhold Niebuhr, Augustine, Thomas Aquinas, Walter Rauschenbusch, and many others. I would stress the strong influence of George Kelsey and Benjamin Mays, African American minister-scholars, as well. Ansbro discusses other black scholars, namely, Booker T. Washington, W. E. B. DuBois, Marcus Garvey, and Elijah Muhammad. But he uses these mainly as a "foil" against King's own approach to black freedom. I understand these other black thinkers to be colleagues with King in a common struggle.[7]

Professor George Davis at Crozer introduced King to the liberal tradition in Christian thought. Schleiermacher, Ritschl, Rauschenbusch, and many others were presented as spokespersons for the liberal tradition. King was greatly impressed with this outlook, which stressed the possibility of human progress. His privileged life experience had prepared him to accept this view at face value. However, there was another aspect to King's experience that haunted him. King was concerned about the oppression of black people he had observed.[8] There was an obvious relation between the liberalism of Davis and the personalism of Brightman and DeWolf. This similarity attracted King to Boston University to pursue a PhD.[9]

ROOTS OF RESISTANCE

In an essay on personalism, Rufus Burrow Jr. discusses what he calls King's "homespun personalism." This is what King received in his early life. He then refers to the Boston input as "formal personalism." Burrow then asserts that King went beyond his teachers by becoming "a social activist personalist." Burrow writes: "He spent his entire ministerial vocation applying personalistic principles to practical solutions to the triple menaces of racism, economic exploitation, and militarism."[10]

It is important to distill what King accepted from his encounter with Boston personalism. Burrow provides a convenient summary. First, *person* is prominent both metaphysically and ethically. God loves persons unconditionally, without reference to intellect, racial origin, or social position. Individuals have value because they have value to God. Second, the personalism that attracted King is *theistic*. God is personal and is the creator and sustainer of the created order. This God is infinitely loving, caring, responsive, active, righteous, and just. The universe is under the guidance of a personal and loving creator God. Third, personalism is *"freedomistic."* Humans are personal and free. To be a person is to be an agent capable of acting, whether for good or evil. Persons are self-determined.[11]

This emphasis upon freedom is critical to the essence of being personal. King dwells upon this characteristic of being personal for obvious reasons. Freedom is given with the creation. Some persons are not free because they are mentally retarded or imbecilic. This raises the theodicy question. Some persons are not free moral agents due to the denial of basic life chances. These instances raise moral and sociopolitical questions. All persons who are moral agents are obligated to seek freedom for themselves and others. Freedom, according to King, is crucial to being a person. First, freedom is the capacity to be self-directed. That is, one has the capacity to deliberate or weigh alternatives. Second, freedom expresses itself in decision. Third, freedom implies responsibility. Once a person makes a decision, he or she is responsible for it and the consequences that result. Any practice or action that threatens one's freedom is a block to one's personhood and limits one's ability to weigh alternatives, to make decisions, and to be responsible for choices.[12]

Without freedom, there can be no persons. Without freedom, neither morality nor knowledge is possible, since each depends on the capacity to deliberate and choose. With Edgar Brightman, King agreed that freedom is an abiding expression of the higher spiritual nature of persons.

Finally, personalism conceives of reality as thoroughly relational and communal. The individual never experiences self in total isolation. The self is not complete without communication with other persons. This relationship between the individual and the group points to King's "beloved community" ethic. At our best we are persons "in community."[13]

We must now take a closer look at King's interpretation and use of a nonviolent ethic. If personalism provided a formal entry into a philosophical and theological perspective, nonviolence provided a method to forge social transformation leading to social justice.

John Ansbro gives a substantial discussion to the intellectual quest of King's search for a method to overcome collective evil. Thoreau suggested noncooperation with an evil system. Socrates practiced civil disobedience. Augustine in *De libero arbitrio* declared that an unjust law is a human law that is not based on the eternal law and the natural law. King appeals to the thought of Heraclitus and Hegel to argue for growth through struggle.[14]

King applied his Hegelian insights to the role that Rosa Parks played in initiating the Montgomery protest: "She was a victim of both the forces of history and the forces of destiny. She had been tracked down by the *Zeitgeist*—the spirit of the time."[15]

In 1959, in a farewell sermon to his congregation in Montgomery, King applied his Hegelian insights to that decision. King implied that he had not sought leadership, but had come to realize that he himself was in the grip of the *Zeitgeist*: "I can't stop now. History has thrust something upon me which I cannot turn away. I should free you now."[16] He related this sense of purpose to the freedom experienced by former colonies throughout the world at that time. In this manner, personalism and nonviolence converged in his thinking and activity.

Gandhi's thought and action, based upon the nonviolent ethic, had a pronounced effect on King. Gandhi practiced this ethic first in South Africa and later in India. He used noncooperation and civil disobedience against the British to free his people. King observed Gandhi's thought and practice. However, he realized that Gandhi's nonviolent ethic needed to be modified in order to be effective in reaching racial justice in this country.[17] Some of the differences between King and Gandhi in method stemmed from the fact that Gandhi was seeking independence from an alien system, while King's goal was the transformation of the structures of the existing system so that all citizens could experience freedom within the system.[18]

THE PILGRIMAGE TO NONVIOLENCE

William D. Watley provides an excellent summary of the elements that made up King's nonviolent ethic.[19] First, King asserted that nonviolence as a means for social change is a method for the strong and not for the cowardly. If one turns to nonviolence due to fear or a lack of the instruments of violence, one is not truly nonviolent. Nonviolence should not be confused with passivity since it involves active resistance King viewed nonviolent action as spiritual; one resists in this manner with love rather than hate.

Second, the goal of nonviolent action is redemption and reconciliation. The use of nonviolence in opposing evil is not humiliation or defeat. It is focused upon winning the enemy's friendship and understanding. The aftermath of violence, on the contrary, is bitterness, hatred, and brokenness. The nonviolent resister may use boycotts and noncooperation as a means to achieve appropriate social change. When oppressed people seek justice, the response may be violent. Nevertheless, King believed that there needs to be this "creative tension" to unearth and overcome injustice in a status quo situation. When King was opposed by the religious leaders of Birmingham, he reminded them that he had been invited and that he was there because injustice was there.

Third, the opponent is the symbol of a greater evil. King depersonalized the target of the nonviolent resister's attack. The opponent is a symbol of a greater evil. Nonviolence is to be directed against the forces of evil rather than against the persons who commit the evil. Evildoers are victims of evil as much as are the individuals and communities that the evildoers oppress. King saw the tension in Montgomery as more than the white-black situation. The real tension, as he viewed it, was between justice and injustice.

Some may raise questions on King's position at this point. Reinhold Niebuhr believed that individuals may be more evil as part of a group with an evil purpose. Nevertheless, the individual participating in the evil action must be held accountable. The success King had in opposing the evil of segregation came when he was able to target a person who was a leader in an oppressive situation. Bull Connor, who jailed and hosed down women and children in Birmingham, is a prime example.

Fourth, King advocated the principle that nonviolence that leads to suffering has redemptive meaning. King's assumption was about power. He assumed that there is social and economic power in noncooperation and that moral power comes in voluntary suffering for others. The nonviolent resister has to be able to accept suffering without retaliating and accept blows without striking back. King believed that unearned suffering has both educational possibilities and redemptive benefits. One can only hold this assumption if one has a confessional affinity with King. By the time he wrote *Strength to Love*, King had been through much personal suffering. He had been imprisoned twelve times. His home had been bombed twice, and he had been the victim of a near fatal stabbing. He could have reacted with bitterness, or he could have sought to transform his suffering into a creative force. He chose the latter course.

Fifth, *agape* was the central principle of King's nonviolent ethic. The non-violent resister must avoid external physical violence and internal violence of the spirit. This love ethic has to be at the center of one's life if the nonviolent approach to opposing evil is to be effective. By love, King did not mean sentimentality or affectionate emotion. King had in mind the love ethic of the New Testament. He defined *agape* as "understanding, redeeming goodwill for all persons." It is a purely spontaneous, unmotivated, groundless love. It is not aroused by any quality or function of its objects but is the love of God operating in the human heart.

It is difficult for secular-minded persons to comprehend what King meant by love. He did not obtain in his efforts the total absence of egoistic aspirations. It is therefore essential that we look upon his understanding of love as an ideal—a reach beyond our grasp. He understood it as the power of God operating in the human heart. He observed that it is this power of God rather than human intuition that makes *agape* conceivable, operable, and potentially attainable. Grounding his ethic of love in theological terms became a problem for King during his final protests. We will visit that situation soon.

Many civil rights organizations, labor unions, and other groups devoted to worthy causes have used the nonviolent technique to get concrete results. Court injunctions, strikes, sit-ins, and other tactics have been effective independently of this love ethic. Activists may see love as an enhancement but not as a requirement. However, the expression of love through nonviolence was for King a faith claim, a way of life, and not merely a way of action. He remained devoted to a ministry of reconciliation with justice. His goal was the creation of the beloved community.[20]

Watley concludes his summary by identifying a sixth principle in King's nonviolent philosophy, based upon his acceptance of theological liberalism. King held the conviction that the universe is on the side of justice. This conviction gives the nonviolent resister faith in the future and strength to accept suffering without retaliation. King reasoned that even if one did not believe in a personal God, one might believe in a creative force in the universe that worked for "universal wholeness."

As we ponder the components of King's nonviolent ethic, we can see more clearly why and how he was able to "speak truth to power." Throughout his life his ethical point of view matured and deepened. He wrestled with truth and he witnessed a deepening of his faith as he moved steadily toward the fulfillment of a life of witness before God and for others.

KING'S NIGHTMARE AND MARTYRDOM

After Selma, King's assessment of the racial situation and his approach to social transformation acquired a new look.[21] He was especially disturbed by the death of four black girls in a church bombing in Birmingham. This tragic event occurred on September 15, 1963, just two weeks after the "I Have a Dream" speech. King, together with his aides, met with President John F. Kennedy at the White House on September 19. This encounter with the president was encouraging; however, this developing relationship came to a sudden end with the assassination of Kennedy on November 22.

King had eulogized the four girls who had been killed while in Sunday school at Birmingham's Sixteenth Street Baptist Church. He described them as "martyred heroines" of the crusade for freedom and human dignity. He assured the bereaved congregation that they "did not die in vain." He concluded his sermon by stating that "God still has a way of wringing good out of evil." He added a statement of significance for his nonviolent ethic: "Unmerited suffering is redemptive."[22]

King was deeply moved by the loss of Kennedy. He considered Kennedy a courageous man and described him as "a friend of civil rights and a stalwart advocate of peace." King warned that "this virus of hate . . . will lead inevitably to our moral and spiritual doom."[23] King felt deeply the loss of a great national leader. He also saw Kennedy's death as an omen of his own death. He observed that hate is contagious and spreads like a disease. Racism was like a cancer that spread through the nation's life. King recalled the murder of Medgar Evers in Mississippi as well as the four girls in Alabama as evidence of the sickness of the society. Nevertheless, he was more determined than ever to continue to witness for freedom and justice.[24]

King's persistent struggle for freedom continued as he was invited to various trouble spots. One such place was St. Augustine, Florida. When hundreds of demonstrators for civil rights were jailed there on May 28, 1964, King appealed for outside help. King himself was arrested on June 11. A biracial committee was formed. On July 2, 1964, President Lyndon Johnson, a southerner, signed the Civil Rights Act of 1964. King described this as "a legislative achievement of rare quality." He commented that this legislation "was first written in the streets." King was encouraged by the support the act received from Congress and the president. However, he felt that much more needed to be accomplished if blacks were to be free.[25]

The riots in Watts had opened King's eyes regarding the challenge racism presented in the North as well as the West. The situation for blacks in the North made it plain that racism and economic injustice had to be attacked at the same time. Politics had to be considered also. At this point, King moved

his family into the slums of Chicago. His wife joined him first. When his children came, he noted that their behavior changed for the worse, almost immediately, and so he sent them back to Atlanta.

Lawndale, where the Kings lived, was an island of poverty. Children were
pleased to have someone say hello to them. They lived in a world where their
parents were often forced to ignore them. Both parents had to work long
hours, and responsible fathers held two jobs, one by day and another at night.
Neighbors paid more rent to live in the slums than whites paid for modern
apartments in the suburbs.

King described the situation as a type of internal colonialism. The colony was
powerless because important decisions were made outside the community. Daily
life was dominated by the welfare worker and policeman. The profits of landlord and merchant were removed and seldom if ever reinvested in the ghetto.

King's effort in Chicago revealed that there was a serious problem in race
relations that needed to be addressed. The staff of the SCLC, however, was in
unknown territory. Staff persons had not been prepared for what King faced.
Many young blacks had not been brought up in the church, and they were prepared to turn to violence to change their situation. The attempt to make
Chicago an open city seemed hopeless.[26]

The mayor of Chicago, Richard J. Daley, was not very helpful. His relationship to King was purely political. When King offered a project, Daley
"outfoxed" him by making some changes and receiving credit for them. His
use of political power to bring equality did not prove to be substantial. Thus,
King's effort was beset by many setbacks.

A special relationship to Jews unfolded in Chicago. When King focused his
campaign on housing, he encountered many Jews. This was the result of rent
strikes on the West Side. In most instances, the strikes were against Jewish
landlords. The West Side had been a Jewish ghetto, but as large numbers of
blacks had flooded in from the South, especially Mississippi, the Jewish residents moved out. King himself had a Jewish landlord. He discovered that the
same Jewish landlords were charging blacks more rent for their apartments in
the slums than they were charging whites for the sanitary, nice, new rooms in
Grant Park. The difference was 20 percent; King referred to this differential
as a "color tax." This difference in assessment was levied by Jewish storekeepers as well as landlords.

This revelation was very painful to King. Some of his best supporters in the
civil rights efforts in the South had been Jewish businesspersons and rabbis.[27]
This negative relationship between blacks and Jews appeared to be a northern
ghetto phenomenon. King met Jews in dissimilar roles. On the one hand, he
knew Jews as among his most committed and generous partners in the civil
rights struggle. On the other hand, in Chicago, he met them as exploitative

landlords and gouging storekeepers. King considered these Jewish exploiters as operating out of the ethics of marginal business entrepreneurs rather than from religious Jewish ethics. Nevertheless, this distinction that King was able to assess was not shared by blacks who endured this victimization.

King learned much about racial discrimination at a fundamental level in Chicago. He completed *Where Do We Go from Here?* in Chicago.[28]

In his final years of witness against collective evil, King faced four issues: "black power," Vietnam, poverty, and his own death. We will consider each of these briefly.

As we attempt to assess the meaning of black power in the struggle for racial justice, we need to say something about the role of the Black Muslims. Elijah Muhammad advocated the separation of the black and white races. He felt that whites were inherently evil and therefore asserted that efforts at integration of the races were hypocritical. He opposed King's use of love in this context. The view of Elijah was that King's philosophy, based upon love and nonviolence, was a "slave philosophy." He believed that blacks had the right to defend themselves, violently. Nonviolent action, advocated by King, was viewed as immoral. Still, both groups were seeking justice and equality.[29] King himself saw something positive in the Black Muslim movement. He observed that the Muslims had rehabilitated ex-convicts and dope addicts (both men and women) who, through despair and self-hatred, had sunk to the level of moral degeneracy.[30]

Black power became a real challenge to King's nonviolent program, especially after its slogan was inserted into the civil rights movement itself. A coalition of civil rights organizations, including the Student Nonviolent Coordinating Committee (SNCC) and the Congress of Racial Equality (CORE), had come together to support King and the Southern Christian Leadership Conference (SCLC). Stokely Carmichael of SNCC and Floyd McKissick of CORE were with King to complete a march through Mississippi after James Meredith was shot in June 1966. During a rally in Greenwood, Mississippi, Carmichael made a call for "black power."

Thus, a disagreement surfaced between King and other groups in this loose coalition. King felt he had to take a stand. He had been put in a defensive position by the students and their leaders. At first, he reflected upon the negative values of this slogan. He viewed it as stemming from a nihilistic philosophy born of the conviction that African Americans cannot win. It implied separation of the races, and it called for retaliatory violence.

He knew that there was much despair in the ranks of the civil rights movement. Blacks were tired of being beaten and jailed for attempting to exercise their constitutional rights. In the meantime, the black masses were being denied the freedoms that the civil rights movement had supposedly gained. This was mainly due to economic injustices.

Against this background, we can observe King's genius as a thinker. He began by defining "power," and then poured content into its meaning. Power, he declared, is the achievement of purpose.[31] It can be exercised for either good or evil goals. He commented that power without love is reckless and abusive, and that love without power is sentimental and anemic. He reasoned further that love that does not satisfy justice is not real love. It is merely a sentimental affection. Love is at its best when justice is concretized. He went on to assert that what blacks want are good jobs, good education, decent homes, and a share of power.[32]

We now turn to King's opposition to war and specifically to the war in Vietnam. This prophetic position was very costly to King. He lost support for civil rights from friends and foes. Leaders in the civil rights movement openly opposed him. Whitney Young, head of the Urban League, was very outspoken in this matter. Liberal whites backed away from the movement. President Johnson was very much opposed to King's views on the war. Some who agreed with King feared a mix of peace with civil rights. They wanted to make more progress and were of the opinion that King's peace efforts were antithetical to the freedom struggle.

King believed that his role as a Nobel Prize winner made the struggle for peace in the world a part of his destiny as a moral leader. He had arrived at the view that all human life is interdependent in a global sense. The modern weapons of warfare had led him to his earlier view that sometimes war is a negative good, used to restrain a tyrant. He now believed that war is obsolete. We must opt for peace. We must find an alternative to war or humans will destroy themselves. The choice we face is nonviolence or nonexistence, as he viewed the situation.[33]

In November 1967, at a meeting of the SCLC, King called for a radical redistribution of economic and political power. During that meeting, King made a decision that the SCLC would organize and lead waves of the nation's poor and disinherited to Washington, DC, in the spring of 1968 to demand redress of their grievances by the United States government and to secure jobs or income for all. King looked back to successful campaigns as he looked forward to this new thrust for social justice, for blacks and for the poor in general. Selma and Birmingham were in mind. He was concerned about millions of poor people who were imprisoned by exploitation and discrimination. These poor—which included not only African Americans but also Native Americans, Mexican Americans, Puerto Ricans, Appalachians, and others—would be invited to participate in the Poor People's Campaign.[34]

King considered the findings of the National Advisory Commission of Civil Disorders, that America is divided between two hostile societies and that the chief destructive cutting edge is racism. King would invite all persons of goodwill to support this effort at social transformation. King had come to the conclusion that those seeking freedom and justice could not depend upon government initiative. They must find a way to apply pressure. King had learned from past demonstrations that he needed a focus to be effective. Therefore, for this campaign, he would place the issues of jobs and income before the decision makers in Washington. He put the matter this way: "The American people are infected with racism—that is the peril. Paradoxically, they are also infected with democratic ideals—that is our hope."[35] King let it be known that this was a faith-inspired activity:

> Jesus was a serious man precisely because he dealt with the tang of the human amidst the glow of the Divine, and that he was concerned about their problems. He was concerned about bread; he opened and started Operation Breadbasket a long time ago. He initiated the first sit-in movement. The greatest revolutionary that history has ever known. And when people tell us when we stand up that we got our inspiration from this or that, go back and let them know where we got our inspiration.[36]

King had long ago come to the conclusion that racism is a systemic evil; therefore, the society needed to be not merely changed but transformed. Racism, as he now believed, was so deeply entrenched that it was unconscious. From this perspective, he now deepened and broadened his efforts to include economic goals. The fight against racism was now threefold—racism, militarism, and economic injustice. His tactic was now civil disobedience. His goal would be to shut down the federal government until changes were made to liberate the oppressed in this country. His plan was "revolutionary in intent." King made it clear that he was exercising the revolutionary edge of Christianity. He declared, "You don't have to go to Karl Marx to learn how to be a revolutionary. I didn't get my inspiration from Karl Marx; I got it from a man named Jesus, a Galilean saint who said he was anointed to heal the brokenhearted. He was anointed to deal with the problems of the poor."[37]

TOWARD THE END

In March 1968, King made about thirty-five speeches. He had been to Detroit, where he made four speeches, and to Los Angeles, where he had spoken five times. He also preached three times in churches in Los Angeles. He flew from Los Angeles to Memphis, where he took up the cause of sanitation workers.

One thousand three hundred sanitation workers were on strike in Memphis. He spoke to these workers to let them know that he identified with their situation. He indicated that all labor has dignity. He urged them to stick together and exercise the power in their protest. King urged them not to give in to the authorities until their demands were met. Power, he reminded them, is the ability to achieve purpose. Freedom is not something voluntarily given by the oppressor. It must be demanded by the oppressed. His concluding remarks were those of a prophet-preacher. Using the parable of Lazarus and Dives, he discussed poverty and wealth. His purpose was to help his hearers understand the justice in their struggle. His final remarks point to how he viewed his witness in Memphis. It is as if he knew that his struggle for freedom would end there.

> Having to live under the threat of death everyday, sometimes I feel discouraged. Having to take so much abuse and criticism, sometimes from my own people, sometimes I feel discouraged. Having to go to bed so often frustrated with the chilly winds of adversity about to stagger me, sometimes I feel discouraged and feel my work's in vain.
>
> But then the Holy Spirit revives my soul again. In Gilead, there is a balm to make the wounded whole. If we believe that, we will build a new Memphis.[38]

There is meaning in King's death that flows from his life. Here the observation from existentialism is appropriate. Existentialist philosophers have asserted that one cannot evaluate a person's life until it ends. As we look back upon the various stages of King's life, one cannot help but be impressed with what he was able to do in such a short period of time.

King had a very profound view of history and his own purpose for living within it. His study of Hegel's philosophy of history served him well. He believed that he was caught up in what he called the *Zeitgeist*, or spirit of the times.[39] He viewed his call to ministry as a summons to help others.[40] Frederick Downing, who has studied King's life from the perspective of James Fowler's "stages of life," sees King as a "religious genius" and observes that "Martin had felt a mystical identity with the spirit and meaning of Christ's passion."[41] As King's wife reflected upon the meaning of his death, she further saw meaning in the fact that his death occurred during the Easter season.[42] When she heard of her husband's death, she was not surprised. The reason she expected his death was obvious. King had lived under the threat of death for many years. Now that he was dead, she had to attempt to grasp some meaning from this tragic event.[43]

As early as his brief pastorate at Dexter Avenue Baptist Church in Montgomery, King indicated that he had come to terms with the possibility of personal death. In a sermon on love as the antidote to fear, he declared, "But though death is inevitable, we do not fear it. . . . Death is not the ultimate evil; the ultimate evil is to be outside God's love."[44]

Another existentialist observation is that it is easier to discuss the death of someone else than it is to consider one's own death. King was able to conquer the fear of death to such an extent that he conveyed the possibility of his own death to his audiences. Thus, his purpose in life was to "do God's will" in seeking justice for the "'least of these,' among humans the world over." This in essence was the meaning of his life and death.

King reflected specifically on his own death with these words: "Every now and then I think about my own death, and I think about my own funeral. . . . Every now and then I ask myself, What would you want said? . . . I'd like somebody to mention that day, that Martin Luther King, Jr. tried to give his life serving others." He then added a request: "Say that I was a drum major for justice. Say that I was a drum major for righteousness."[45]

Listen to his final words in Memphis:

> Well, I don't know what will happen now. . . . But it doesn't matter to me now, because I have been to the mountain top. . . . I would like to live a long life—longevity has its place. But I'm not concerned about that now. I just want to do God's will. And He's allowed me to go up to the mountain. And I've looked over, and I've seen the Promised Land. I may not get there with you. But I want you to know tonight, that we, as a people, will get to the Promised Land.[46]

Conclusion

The Presence of the Kingdom of God

We come now to the summary and conclusion of our study. I believe that the following words from the Lord's Prayer capture the spirit behind the life, thought, witness, and death of Bonhoeffer and King: "Thy kingdom come, Thy will be done, on earth as it is in heaven" (Matt. 6:10). The entire Sermon on the Mount was venerated by both theologians. They gleaned a message of love, justice, and hope from the words of Jesus in that great biblical message. In chapter 9 we saw how Gandhi, Bonhoeffer, and King received inspiration from this portion of the Bible.

As we launch a brief comparison of the witness of Bonhoeffer and King to social justice, we remember that they both reflected up the means to bring the presence of God's kingdom to this world.

As I ponder the lives and witness of both theologians, I am reminded of the title of the film "Heaven Can Wait." Both leaders spoke out against a vertical-only view of religious faith. They were in concert with recent political theologians who have stressed the horizontal outreach of faith. They also anticipated the emphasis in liberation theologies that see the focus upon dogmas and creeds as the second order of business for theologians. In this vein, the emphasis of racial justice in both of our theologians as well as the earthward direction in their ethical concerns was ahead of its time in theological reflection and application. Let us keep these initial reflections in mind as we summarize the findings in this study.

The message of love is essential in the thought of both theologians. The chapter on "love in action" discussed this aspect of their project in some detail. Both King and Bonhoeffer stress the contribution of Christian theological history in their treatment of the love ethic of the Christian faith. They both refer to the Greek philosophical tradition as well as the biblical record. King compares the love ethic of Jesus with the truth ethic of Gandhi. Both appeal to the school of Lutheran theologians at Lund, especially Nygren. My view is that both omitted an important theologian who has influenced much of theological history since his time: Augustine. I believe Augustine's view, which he called *caritas*, is crucial to a Christian view of love. Augustine rooted his understanding of love in what he called *amor Dei* (the love of God). Love of self and love of others are ultimately grounded in the love of God. I find this helpful in leading to the ethical goals that Bonhoeffer and King have in view. It seems to me that this theological "love triangle" provides a meaningful bridge between love and justice. This connection is crucial when love is put in the service of justice as King and Bonhoeffer intend. This provides a humane view of power.

Another crucial concern that King and Bonhoeffer share is an understanding of sinful social structures. We may refer to collective evil or systemic evil in this regard.

Bonhoeffer and King launched their theological program in a context of liberalism. Along the way, each met an older colleague who reminded him of dimensions to evil that he in his youthful outlook had not yet considered. Bonhoeffer met Karl Barth and King encountered the thought of Reinhold Niebuhr. Niebuhr related to both King and Bonhoeffer in their two contexts. He even taught Bonhoeffer, but his influence appears to have been limited to introducing his German student to black music and literature during Bonhoeffer's study at Union Theological Seminary in New York. Niebuhr's attempt to get Bonhoeffer out of Germany in 1939 needs to be noted. However, his impact on King had theological and ethical substance. His influence upon King was much like a conversion from liberalism (focused upon belief in the inevitability of human progress toward the good life) to realism (regarding human sinfulness, especially in social groups). Niebuhr helped King to deal with the systemic evil of racism that was his main concern.

When we consider the depth and breadth of collective evil, one needs to begin to take seriously the relationship between love and justice. As King reminds us, evil is real and aggressive, and requires a struggle on our part to transform the social unit that sponsors it.

Bonhoeffer was just as committed as King in opposing collective evil in his situation. Nevertheless, he faced special odds. First, he had to modify the "two kingdoms" view of his Lutheran background. Second, his context was a situation of anti-Semitism, even among leading church figures and theologians. This limited his use of the Old Testament. He was cautious about the doctrine of creation, since theologians among the German Christians had corrupted this doctrine to argue for the superiority of Aryans as a race. For Bonhoeffer, the Old Testament was the book of Christ. He did not seem free to accept the authenticity of the message of the Hebrew Scriptures. He said little about the Hebrew prophets of social justice.

King had an obvious advantage in his free use of the entire Bible together with the best biblical criticism and interpretation available to him. King also was anchored in the thought of the black Baptist tradition as well as the tradition of the radical wing of the Reformation. King clearly viewed the church as the conscience of the state. I am reminded of my study of the Cambridge Platonists,[1] who declared that "the author of nature is the giver of grace." In this view, creation and redemption are brought together. King's support from the Old Testament for the message of love in the New Testament is linked in his view by the words of Amos: "Let justice roll down like waters, and righteousness like an everflowing stream" (Amos 5:24). King's movement from Amos to Jesus brought love and justice together in his understanding.

Christology is central to the thought of both theologians. Biblical passages such as Matthew 22:37–40 and Luke 4:18 represent the outlook of both theologians. The first passage speaks of love of God, self, and neighbor. The second passage is a call to serve the oppressed. The words and deeds of Jesus are central to both theologians, who desired to bring the virtues of the kingdom of God to humans on this earth.

King agreed with much that Bonhoeffer said about Jesus Christ. However, King had a very low Christology. He shared a Christology from below with Bonhoeffer, but he seemed preoccupied with the human Jesus. I believe that this comes from the influence of Howard Thurman. King is said to have carried Thurman's *Jesus and the Disinherited* with him as he traveled from place to place.[2]

Bearing the cross is important to both King and Bonhoeffer. King puts it this way: "When I took up the cross, I recognized its meaning. . . . The cross is something that you bear, and ultimately that you die on."[3] A similar statement is found in Bonhoeffer's distinction between "cheap" and "costly" grace in the beginning of his *Cost of Discipleship*.[4]

In his nonviolent projects, King emphasized the meaning of "redemptive suffering." This was difficult to sell to young people who were in the civil rights movement without a profound belief in the tenets of the Christian faith. It must also have been unconvincing to older blacks who had spent a lifetime in one form of suffering after another. This belief also had its shortcomings in that it placed almost all of the emphasis upon loving others. King's followers must have inquired, "What about me?" The love ethic that advocates the love of others, as one loves oneself, requires self-respect and a sense of personal dignity that is God-given and that does not depend upon human bestowal. Some unmerited suffering is the result of human bigotry and a sense of superiority based upon race or class. Such social evil needs to meet vigorous opposition, even if it is nonviolent. Some evil exists because there is an indifference to our moral condition in the natural order. However, some human suffering, like slavery and the Holocaust, is the result of human wickedness. The question remains: Which suffering is redemptive? King was able to make this assumption so definite because nonviolent action had become for him "a way of life," regardless of the consequences of his action. George Kelsey, one of King's teachers at Morehouse, wrote a disturbing book, *Racism and the Christian Understanding of Man*, in which he declared:

> Racism is a faith. It is a form of idolatry. . . . It arose as an ideological justification for the constellations of political and economic power which were expressed in colonialism and slavery. . . . The alleged superior race became and now persists as the center of value and an object of devotion. . . . Multitudes. . . . gain their sense of the "power of being" from their membership in the superior race.[5]

This observation by Kelsey is confirmed in the experience of Bonhoeffer and King in their struggles for social justice. The depth of collective evil centering on racism and Nazism was so profound that they found it difficult to explain and confront it. This explains why their reflections on it do not always reach the level of a rationally consistent analysis. The meaning of the cross at the center of the Christian faith affirms that Christ had confronted the evils to which Bonhoeffer and King were heirs. Through Christ's resurrection, there was a witness to the power to overcome sin, evil, and death. In my judgment, neither theologian lifted up the importance of the Christian belief in the resurrection and the guidance and power of the Holy Spirit in their theological perspectives. To effectively witness against the powers of evil, Christians need all the "resources of grace" in their struggle. When one takes a close look at collective evil, one realizes that more than natural circumstances may be responsible for one's suffering. In order to overcome such evils, one needs to distinguish between the causes for one's suffering. If the suffering is due to the inhumanity of humans to each other, one should not see redemption in all of this. Other suffering may be redemptive, and one can use some suffering as a source of moral strength.

Both theologians had a strong sense of community. King majored in sociology at Morehouse College. This provided a solid foundation for his social outreach. He put his notion of community into theological terms. He had much to say about human interdependence. He believed that no one is fulfilled alone; human wholeness comes when there is a strong I-thou relationship based upon love in the quest for justice. Persons in relationship to other persons are essential for any positive group life. This is true for the church as the body of Christ.

Bonhoeffer also made community essential for his view of Christian fellow-ship and the very nature of the church, which has its reason for existence in its "being for others." He described the church as a collective person. The church, according to Bonhoeffer, is Christ "existing as community." It follows that the affirmation of community is at the heart of Bonhoeffer's theological ethic.

The exaltation of the essence of community is an essential piece of common ground for Bonhoeffer and King. It follows that the dignity of per-sons, individual and social, is essential to understanding their theological ethics as well.

Both theologians were on a quest for social justice. They were engaged in an aggressive attack upon the inhuman use of power. Our focus throughout this study has emphasized the meaning of a just use of power to secure human fulfillment, personal and social. King had to take the concept of power seri-ously as he faced the challenge of "black power" advocates in the civil rights movement. This was especially true as he took his movement into northern cities. The masses of people in the "dark ghettos" of this region had not received the benefits of the gains for human dignity evident in the South. In the North, many embittered youth had not had the benefits of education. They often did not have any connection with wholesome family or church relations. They now wanted freedom and the benefits of American democracy. As they lived on the edge of survival, they wanted progress in race relations "by any means necessary."

King attempted to define power in this context in a positive light. He asserted that power is the fulfillment of purpose. Power can be used to obtain good or evil purposes. He affirmed that economic and political power should be used to change conditions. However, his view was that the use of power should be nonviolent.

Bonhoeffer found that he needed to be concerned about the use and abuse of power in Nazi Germany. He became committed to the freedom of the Jew-ish people, the oppressed in his social situation. He was concerned about the weak and powerless in Germany. There were homosexuals, the physically and mentally impaired, and the Gypsies in the society. But the "Jewish question" was that which led him into power politics. He was more aggressive than his colleagues in the Confessing Church, which he helped to organize to oppose the German Christians, who used their religious and church resources to sup-port Hitler. Bonhoeffer was concerned for the welfare of Jews within and with-out the church. He affirmed their humanity and the right for dignified treatment because they were children of God. The common witness of Bon-hoeffer and King in this effort is obvious. Our study has provided a perspec-tive on this concern. Both are worthy of praise for their dedication to the realization of the rights of all persons in their midst and beyond.

In words that point toward the future, Bonhoeffer and King appear to anticipate their own legacy. They leave what I would call "open questions." Bonhoeffer refers to "the meaning of Christ for us today." He asks, "Are we still of any use?"[6] King speaks of "the beloved community" and "the promised land." He wrote a book titled *Where Do We Go from Here?* By such questions, both men appear to be suggesting that they have set us on a good path, but that much more needs to be done by those who take up their witness.

So much evil exists in our time and place that a serious reflection upon their "witness unto death" is greatly needed. In their time and place, Bonhoeffer and King were on a quest for the presence of the kingdom of God on earth. They knew that the kingdom of God is both present and future. It is present when the will of God is done. But it is absent when evil prevails. They gave their all in the effort to realize the ethics of the kingdom, here and now, as much as possible.[7] This we may refer to as "a social eschatology." Ethics and eschatology converge in their view of the purpose of human life, thought, and action in our time and place. In remembrance of their legacy, we repeat their longing in the words of Jesus:

> Thy kingdom come,
> Thy will be done,
>   On earth as it is in heaven.

Notes

Chapter 1: Introduction

1. Lerone Bennett, "When the Man and the Hour Are Met," *Martin Luther King, Jr.: A Profile*, ed. C. Eric Lincoln, rev. ed. (New York: Hill & Wang, 1970), 1–39.
2. Though I had specialized in the philosophy of religion (STM, Hartford Theological Seminary), and philosophical theology (Edinburgh), I taught in other areas as well, namely, Christian ethics, psychology of religion, and comparative religion. In view of my pastoral experience, I was appointed during my first two years at Howard as director of field education. I placed and supervised seminarians in Washington and Baltimore, keeping me connected with pastors and congregations.

   At thirty-one, I faced an unusual challenge. I was mindful of the high standards set by the older generation of black scholars at Howard University. Howard Thurman had taught philosophy of religion and was dean of the chapel. Benjamin E. Mays had been dean of the school of religion and professor of theology. Mordecai Johnson was president. William Stuart Nelson was senior professor of philosophy of religion and vice president of the university.

   All these scholars of religion, as well as well-known scholars such as E. Franklin Frazier (sociology), Sterling Brown (literature), and Raford Logan (historian), were on campus. I was the only person teaching systematic theology at that time. Howard was known in those days as "the Black Harvard." When persons ask me if I marched with King, I remind them of my heavy teaching and leadership responsibilities at the Howard University School of Religion.
3. See J. Deotis Roberts, *Black Theology in Dialogue* (Philadelphia: Westminster Press, 1987), chap. 9.
4. See Eberhard Bethge, *Dietrich Bonhoeffer* (New York: Macmillan, 1971), 158.
5. These remarks came from John Godsey of Wesley Theological Seminary. Godsey has produced one of the most important studies available in English on Bonhoeffer. He did his work on Bonhoeffer under Karl Barth.

   The group of Bonhoeffer scholars in the United States who are members of the International Bonhoeffer Society (English language section) have recently given Bonhoeffer his due. Being in dialogue with them has been extremely helpful in my quest for a deeper understanding of Bonhoeffer's life and witness.
6. Jack Forstman, *Christian Faith in Dark Times* (Louisville, KY: Westminster John Knox Press, 1992).
7. See my chapter in David E. Goatley, ed., *Black Religion, Black Theology: The Collected Essays of J. Deotis Roberts* (Harrisburg, PA: Trinity Press International, 2003).

8. James W. McClendon Jr., *Biography as Theology: How Life Stories Can Remake Today's Theology* (Nashville: Abingdon Press, 1974).
9. See my *Black Theology in Dialogue*, chap. 1.

Chapter 2: Biography as Theology

1. Elizabeth Raum, *Dietrich Bonhoeffer: Called by God* (New York: Continuum, 2002), 26.
2. Vincent Harding, *Martin Luther King: The Inconvenient Hero* (Maryknoll, NY: Orbis Books, 1996).
3. See *Dietrich Bonhoeffer: Life in Pictures*, ed. Eberhard and Renate Bethge and Christian Gremmels (Philadelphia: Fortress Press, 1986), 7–9, 32–48. Cf. "The Bonhoeffer Family Tree," ed. Kathy Lancaster, *Church and Society* 85, no. 6 (1995): 8–9. Also see Renate Bethge's essay, "The Memory of a Child," in *The Shame and the Sacrifice: The Life and Martyrdom of Dietrich Bonhoeffer*, by Edwin Robertson (New York: Collier Books, 1988), 11–20.
4. Clayborne Carson, ed., *The Autobiography of Martin Luther King, Jr.* (New York: Warner Books, 1998), 2–3. Cf. Martin Luther King Sr., with Clayton Riley, *Daddy King: An Autobiography* (New York: William Morrow & Co., 1980), 23–36.
5. King and Riley, *Daddy King*, 37–48.
6. Carson, ed., *Autobiography of Martin Luther King, Jr.*, 4–5.
7. Ibid.
8. Ibid., 13. Cf. Lewis V. Baldwin, *There Is a Balm in Gilead: The Cultural Roots of Martin Luther King, Jr.* (Minneapolis: Fortress Press, 1991); and Frederick L. Downing, *To See the Promised Land: The Faith Pilgrimage of Martin Luther King, Jr.* (Macon, GA: Mercer University Press, 1987).

Chapter 3: Academic and Spiritual Growth

1. The most extensive account is Eberhard Bethge, *Dietrich Bonhoeffer: A Biography*, rev. ed. (Minneapolis: Fortress Press, 2000). See also the following: Sabine Leibholz-Bonhoeffer, *The Bonhoeffers: Portrait of a Family* (Chicago: Covenant Publications, 1994); Elizabeth Raum, *Dietrich Bonhoeffer: Called by God* (New York: Continuum, 2002); Edwin Robertson, *The Shame and the Sacrifice: The Life and Martyrdom of Dietrich Bonhoeffer* (New York: Collier Books, 1988).
2. In reference to King's life, I recommend the following: Clayborne Carson, ed., *The Autobiography of Martin Luther King, Jr.* (New York: Warner Books, 1998); Lewis V. Baldwin, *There Is a Balm in Gilead: The Cultural Roots of Martin Luther King, Jr.* (Minneapolis: Fortress Press, 1991); Frederick L. Downing, *To See the Promised Land* (Macon, GA: Mercer University Press, 1986); Martin Luther King Sr., *Daddy King: An Autobiography* (New York: William Morrow & Co., 1980).

Chapter 4: Formative Experiences in Ministry

1. See Elizabeth Raum, *Dietrich Bonhoeffer: Called by God* (New York: Continuum, 2002), 49–77.
2. Clayborne Carson, ed., *The Autobiography of Martin Luther King, Jr.* (New York: Warner Books, 1998), 5. Cf. Lewis V. Baldwin, *There Is a Balm in Gilead: The Cultural Roots of Martin Luther King, Jr.* (Minneapolis: Fortress Press, 1991), 124–25. See also chapter 7 in Carson, which describes in detail the events of Montgomery's bus boycott and King's leadership role as president of the Montgomery Improvement Association (MIA).

3. Mary Hull, *Rosa Parks* (New York: Chelsea House, 1994). See also Rosa Parks (with Gregory J. Reed), *Quiet Strength* (Grand Rapids: Zondervan, 1994). I was both pleased and surprised to receive a letter of invitation to become a founding member of the National Campaign for Tolerance, of which Rosa Parks is co-chair. A Well of Tolerance is to be built in Montgomery, Alabama, near Dexter Avenue Baptist Church. The Southern Poverty Law Center is a sponsor of this significant effort in memory of the civil rights movement and its relevance for today.

4. Quoted in Carson, ed., *Autobiography of Martin Luther King, Jr.*, 93.

5. The following books are noteworthy: Ralph David Abernathy, *And the Walls Came Tumbling Down* (New York: Harper & Row, 1989); Taylor Branch, *Parting the Waters* (New York: Simon & Schuster, 1988) and *Pillar of Fire* (New York: Simon & Schuster, 1998); David Garrow, *Bearing the Cross* (New York: Vintage, 1988).

6. During my leadership at ITC, I was very much a part of the continuing witness of the SCLC. On several occasions this organization took a bold position against injustice toward minorities in Atlanta and elsewhere. The spirit of King was yet alive in this witness.

Chapter 5: Major Theological Resources

1. Elizabeth Raum, *Dietrich Bonhoeffer: Called by God* (New York: Continuum, 2002), 49.

2. Ibid., 50.

3. Eberhard Bethge, *Dietrich Bonhoeffer: A Biography*, rev. ed. (Minneapolis: Fortress Press, 2000), 177–86. Bethge describes in detail the various stages of Bonhoeffer's relation to Barth. In spite of some key differences in their thought, Bonhoeffer often sought to defend Barth's views among critics such as Brunner and Gogarten (see Bethge, 179–80). Bonhoeffer attempted, unsuccessfully, to obtain the Titius Chair for Barth, which had been occupied by Schleiermacher.

4. Ibid., 179.

5. Ibid., 184.

6. Ibid.

7. Dietrich Bonhoeffer, *Act and Being*, vol. 2 of *Dietrich Bonhoeffer Works*, ed. Wayne Whitson Floyd Jr., trans. H. Martin Rumscheidt (Minneapolis: Augsburg Fortress, 1996), 90–91, quoted in Andreas Pangritz, *Karl Barth in the Theology of Dietrich Bonhoeffer* (Grand Rapids: Eerdmans, 2000), 26–27.

8. Pangritz, *Karl Barth in the Theology*, 29. An important treatment of Barth's "moral theology" is John Webster, *Barth's Moral Theology* (Grand Rapids: Eerdmans, 1998). Webster attempts to present a case for human action in the thought of Karl Barth. In view of the dialogue between Bonhoeffer and Barth, this book has real value.

9. Kenneth L. Smith and Ira G. Zepp Jr., *Search for the Beloved Community* (Valley Forge, PA: Judson Press, 1998), 24–25. Cf. John J. Ansbro, *Martin Luther King, Jr.: The Making of a Mind* (Maryknoll, NY: Orbis Books, 1982), chap. 1. Cf. Lawrence Edward Carter Sr., *Walking Integrity: Benjamin Elijah Mays, Mentor to Martin Luther King, Jr.* (Macon, GA: Mercer University Press, 1998), 153–214.

10. See Rufus Burrow, "Personalism, the Objective Moral Order and Moral Law in the Work of Martin Luther King, Jr.," in *The Legacy of Martin Luther King, Jr.: The Boundaries of Law, Politics, and Religion*, by Lewis V. Baldwin, with Rufus Burrow Jr. et al. (Notre Dame, IN: University of Notre Dame Press, 2002),

213–51. At this point I will make two observations. First, as an alumnus of the University of Edinburgh (1957), I am pleased that King did not study for his PhD at Edinburgh. He would have acquired a first-rate classical education there. However, it would not have groomed him for a life of social activism. There was no strong program of theological ethics at New College, the University of Edinburgh, at that time. Boston personalism proved to be ideal for his sense of mission. Second, in a Pew Conference some years ago, Professor Stanley Hauerwas presented a paper on Christian ethics in the United States over the last half of the twentieth century. He did not mention King. I was so disappointed that I raised an objection. He responded later by saying that "King made no contribution to the discipline." At that point we had to agree to disagree. As a colleague of his at Duke Divinity School, I never again broached the subject. His reasoning escapes me!

11. I was introduced to personalism at Edinburgh through lectures by Principal John Baillie, my main mentor in philosophical theology. It was his view that God possesses personality in its perfect and complete form. Humans possess personality in a limited and imperfect sense. A similar view was presented by Professor H. H. Farmer at Cambridge University at the time. As a result of this exposure, I was attracted to the writings of Boston personalists such as DeWolf and Knudson. I used their texts, along with other resources, in teaching systematic theology at Howard University. Later, DeWolf became dean of Wesley Seminary in Washington, where we became colleagues. Another Boston theologian, Paul Schelling, joined DeWolf at Wesley also.

12. Martin Luther King Jr., *A Comparison of the Conceptions of God in the Thinking of Paul Tillich and Henry Nelson Wieman* (Ann Arbor, MI: University Microfilms, 1988).

13. Burrow, "Personalism, the Objective Moral Order, and Moral Law," 221.

14. See Martin Luther King Jr., "God Is Able," in *Strength to Love* (Cleveland: Collins/Word Press, 1963), 106–14.

15. Burrow, "Personalism, the Objective Moral Order, and Moral Law," 222.

16. Ibid., 219.

17. Ibid., 223–24.

18. The African saying "Because I am, we are" needs to be carefully assessed. If it implies that the individual is not important and is swallowed up in the group, then it would deny the freedom so dearly prized by King. If, on the other hand, it has to do with what I often refer to as "person-in-community," it would, I believe, be useful in King's understanding of the self being fulfilled in relation to other selves. Ghanaian philosopher Kwame Gyeke agrees. He argues for a form of communitarianism, in which both the individual and community are acknowledged and respected. See his *Tradition and Modernity: Philosophical Reflections on the African Experience* (New York: Oxford University Press, 1997), chap. 2.

19. Burrow, "Personalism, the Objective Moral Order, and Moral Law," 226.

20. Ibid., 227.

21. Ibid.

Chapter 6: Race and Ethnicity

1. See Robert S. Wistrich, *Anti-Semitism: The Longest Hatred* (London: Methuen, 1992), part 1, pp. 3–97. In part 2, the author discusses racism in the United States as a logical comparison. Cf. Alan T. Davis, ed., *Anti-Semitism and the*

Foundations of Christianity (New York: Paulist Press, 1979). In this work, twelve Christian theologians explore the development and dynamics of anti-Semitism within the Christian tradition.

2. Adolf Hitler, *Mein Kampf*, 14th ed. (New York: Reginald E. Hitchcock, 1940), 16.
3. Ibid., 75.
4. Wistrich, *Anti-Semitism*, 39. This author provides a long quote from Martin Luther, which is as full of hate for Jews as any stated by Hitler. The only difference is that Luther left it with the rulers to deal with the Jews according to their wishes. Hitler, on the other hand, carried out his plan to exterminate as many Jews as he could.
5. Eberhard Bethge, "The Holocaust and Christian Anti-Semitism," *Union Seminary Quarterly Review* 33 (Spring/Summer 1977): 143.
6. Slavery reached throughout the Americas. The Iberian nations of Spain and Portugal sponsored slavery in Latin America. Several European nations introduced it in the Caribbean islands.
7. See Coretta Scott King, *My Life with Martin Luther King, Jr.* (New York: Holt, Rinehart & Winston, 1969), chap. 3. In this chapter, the author describes her experience growing up in Alabama. It is much like my own experience growing up in North Carolina during the same period. One later becomes aware that racism is not merely regional; it is nationwide, though it expresses itself in different forms.
8. Martin Luther King Jr., *Where Do We Go from Here: Chaos or Community?* (New York: Harper & Row, 1967), 70.
9. George D. Kelsey, *Racism and the Christian Understanding of Man* (New York: Charles Scribner's Sons, 1965), 24. The full impact of Kelsey's observation, through the use of gender inclusive language, would include white females as well as males. I know Kelsey was passionately concerned about segregation in the churches. He made a crucial observation to me personally: He said the white church is "a segregating church," while the black church is "not segregating though segregated." This difference is important and needs careful consideration by both groups.
10. King, *Where Do We Go from Here?* 75.
11. Ibid., 97. Here we recall that the strong theological objection to racism by Kelsey was the belief in the *imago Dei*, which makes all humans equal. For the same reasons, I have stressed "the dignity of humans" in my *Liberation and Reconciliation: A Black Theology* (Philadelphia: Westminster Press, 1971), chap. 4.
12. Bonhoeffer's second visit was in 1939. He left for Germany within one month due to the situation there.
13. E. H. Robertson, *Dietrich Bonhoeffer* (London: Carey Kingsgate Press, 1966), 17.
14. A close family friend, Paul Ford, who is presently doing graduate study at the Free University of Berlin, has done some research in the Bonhoeffer archives in Berlin. In a recent conversation I had with Paul, he reported that he had discovered a document that reports some of Bonhoeffer's observations in Washington, DC. Bonhoeffer noticed that light-skinned blacks made up most of the middle and upper classes in the black community. This is a profound observation. It goes back to the division between house slaves and field slaves. The light-skinned slaves were usually the sons and daughters of slave masters who had fathered them with female slaves. As a result, many of these persons received educational and economic advantages ahead of blacks with dark skin.

15. See Wil Haygood, *King of the Cats: The Life and Times of Adam Clayton Powell, Jr.* (New York: Houghton Mifflin, 1993), 58–72. Haygood provides a good look at Powell Sr.'s life and ministry. He notes that Germany was a favorite location for Powell Sr. when vacationing in Europe (p. 71).
16. Scott Holland, "First We Take Manhattan, Then We Take Berlin: Bonhoeffer's New York," *Cross Currents* 50, no. 3 (Fall 2000): 373.
17. Ibid., 374.
18. See Josiah Ulysses Young III, *No Difference in the Fare: Dietrich Bonhoeffer and the Problem of Racism* (Grand Rapids: Eerdmans, 1998). This volume, by an African American theologian, provides more comprehensive coverage of Bonhoeffer's encounter with racism in the United States than I am able to provide in this study. According to Young, Bonhoeffer was introduced to the "Black Christ" through the writing of Countee Cullen. At Christmas, during his stay in America, he did serious reflection on the "White Christ" and the "Black Christ." He observed, "If it has come about that today the 'Black Christ' has been led into the field against a 'White Christ' by a Negro poet, then a deep cleft in the church is indicated" (p. 123).
19. Some contend that the experience of Bonhoeffer is still alive in the appreciation Germans have for black music. See Martha Bayles, "Gospel Speaks a Language Germans Understand," *New York Times*, October 21, 2001. I am uneasy about this coverage. First, it appears that most Germans consider black gospel as a form of entertainment rather than a means to worship. In the second place, the concerts are usually in halls of entertainment rather than in churches. Third, they do not seem to know the difference between gospel music and spirituals and the message in each. I shared my observations with a German theologian and his wife, and they were in basic agreement with my assessment.

Chapter 7: Love in Action

1. John D. Godsey, "Bonhoeffer's Doctrine of Love," in *New Studies in Bonhoeffer's Ethics*, ed. William J. Peck, Toronto Studies in Theology 30, Bonhoeffer Series, 5 (Lewiston, NY: Edwin Mellen Press, 1987), 189.
2. Ibid., 206–7.
3. Ibid., 207–8. Cf. Dietrich Bonhoeffer, *The Communion of Saints*, trans. Ronald Gregor Smith et al. (New York: Harper & Row, 1963), 40–44, 118–36, 120–22.
4. Bonhoeffer, *Communion of Saints*, 130.
5. Godsey, "Bonhoeffer's Doctrine of Love," 209.
6. See Dietrich Bonhoeffer, *No Rusty Swords: Letters, Lectures, and Notes from the Collected Works of Dietrich Bonhoeffer*, ed. Edwin H. Robertson, trans. Edwin H. Robertson and John Bowden (London: Collins, 1965), 38–39. In a lecture in Barcelona titled "What Is a Christian Ethic?" Bonhoeffer stated, "There are countless ways from man to God, and therefore there are also countless ethics, but there is only one way from God to man, and that is the way of love in Christ, the way of the cross" (p. 37).
7. Cf. Bonhoeffer's sermon on "Love of God." His text was 1 John 4:16—"God is love, and he who abides in love abides in God, and God abides in him." The sermon was preached to an American audience in English. He urges American Christians and German Christians to love each other and "to build one holy Christianity . . . with God the Father and Christ as Lord and the Holy Spirit as the sanctifying power" (Bonhoeffer, *No Rusty Swords*, 80).

8. Dietrich Bonhoeffer, *Creation and Fall*, trans. John C. Fletcher and Kathleen Downham (New York: Macmillan, 1966), 25, 35, 37–38.

9. Dietrich Bonhoeffer, *Act and Being*, trans. Bernard Noble (New York: Harper & Row, 1962), 90. Bonhoeffer also speaks of God's creation of men and women for a love bond in marriage. He indicates that the fall has endangered this relationship as it has all others among humans (Godsey, "Bonhoeffer's Doctrine of Love," 211–12).

10. Bonhoeffer on several occasions reflects on the meaning of love. He delivered four sermons on 1 Corinthians 13 in the fall of 1934. His essential message was that a church with a true confession and orthodox faith is worthless unless it has a pure, encompassing love abiding in its fellowship. See Dietrich Bonhoeffer, *The Way to Freedom*, ed. E. H. Robertson, trans. E. H. Robertson and John Bowden (London: Collins, 1972), 95. In wedding ceremonies, Bonhoeffer let couples know that in addition to human love, they needed Christian love as a marriage bond. See Bonhoeffer, *Gesammelte Schriften* (Munich: Kaiser Verlag, 1958–1974), 4:463.

11. Godsey, "Bonhoeffer's Doctrine of Love," 216–18.

12. Ibid., 219.

13. Ibid., 220–22.

14. Anders Nygren, *Agape and Eros*, trans. Philip Watson (New York: Harper & Row, 1969).

15. Reinhold Niebuhr, *An Interpretation of Christian Ethics* (New York: Harper & Row, 1935), 211.

16. See Martin Luther King Jr., *Strength to Love* (Cleveland: Collins, 1963), chap. 5. Cf. John Ansbro, *Martin Luther King, Jr.: The Making of a Mind* (Maryknoll, NY: Orbis Books, 1994), 8–9.

17. I have attempted to find a deeper meaning in biblical faith and classical church history. See "The Meaning of Love," in my *Black Theology in Dialogue* (Philadelphia: Westminster Press, 1987), 66–69. See also Donald Dietz, "The Christian Meaning of Love: A Study of the Thought of Anders Nygren" (PhD diss., Pontifica Studiorum Universitas, Rome, 1976). The value of Dietz's study is significant. He has put Nygren's study in the context of Swedish Lutheran research. Cf. Bernard V. Brody, *How Christians through the Ages Have Understood Love* (Washington, DC: Georgetown University Press, 2003). This study is invaluable for its historical perspective. It covers biblical history as well as the Christian movement. Finally, see Stephen G. Post, *Unlimited Love: Altruism, Compassion, and Service* (Philadelphia: Templeton Foundation Press, n.d.). Post attempts to put the study of love in the context of "altruism." He believes a socio-scientific no less than an ethico-theological understanding of love is important. This study is unique and very informative.

18. Ervin Smith, *The Ethics of Martin Luther King, Jr.*, Studies in American Religion 2 (New York: Edwin Mellen Press, 1981), 89–90.

19. Ibid., 90.

20. Quoted in Geffrey B. Kelly and F. Burton Nelson, eds., *A Testament to Freedom: The Essential Writings of Dietrich Bonhoeffer* (San Francisco: HarperSanFrancisco, 1990), 320.

Chapter 8: Confronting Collective Evils

1. John J. Ansbro, *Martin Luther King, Jr.: The Making of a Mind* (Maryknoll, NY: Orbis Books, 1992), 110–11.

2. Reinhold Niebuhr, *Moral Man and Immoral Society* (New York: Charles Scribner's Sons, 1955).
3. Ansbro, *Martin Luther King, Jr.*, 151. I will not be pursuing Reinhold Niebuhr's views here. We will, however, return to him in part 3.
4. Quoted in Ansbro, *Martin Luther King, Jr.*, 160. King borrowed this insight from Henry Nelson Wieman.
5. Martin Luther King Jr., *Strength to Love* (New York: Harper & Row, 1963), 58.
6. Dietrich Bonhoeffer, *Ethics*, ed. Eberhard Bethge (New York: Macmillan, 1955), 18–19.
7. Ibid.
8. Ibid., 19–20.
9. Ibid., 20–26.
10. Geffrey B. Kelly and F. Burton Nelson, eds., *A Testament to Freedom: The Essential Writings of Dietrich Bonhoeffer* (San Francisco: HarperSanFrancisco, 1990), 106–7.
11. Ibid., 105.
12. Wayne Whitson Floyd, *The Wisdom and Witness of Dietrich Bonhoeffer* (Minneapolis: Fortress Press, 2000), 79. Cf. my reflections on collective evil in *Black Theology in Dialogue* (Philadelphia: Westminster Press, 1987), chap. 9.

Chapter 9: The Fellowship of Kindred Minds

1. See K. L. Seshagini Rao, "Gandhi and the Cross," an unpublished paper delivered for the Council for World Religions meeting at Harrison Hot Springs, Canada, August 20–28, 1987.
2. Mohandas Gandhi, "The Message of Jesus," in Robert Ellsberg, ed., *Gandhi on Christianity* (Maryknoll, NY: Orbis Books, 1993), 21. Gandhi gave a talk to Christians who were fellow passengers on a ship going from London to India. They had attended the Second Round Table Conference in London. The date of this talk was Christmas Day, 1931.
3. John Hick, foreword to *Gandhi's Religious Thought*, by Margaret Chatterjee (Notre Dame, IN: University of Notre Dame Press, 1983), ix–xii.
4. Chatterjee, *Gandhi's Religious Thought*, 13.
5. Ibid., 11.
6. Ibid., 13.
7. Eberhard Bethge, *Dietrich Bonhoeffer: A Biography*, rev. ed. (Minneapolis: Fortress Press, 2000), 147.
8. Ibid., 148.
9. Ibid. When Bonhoeffer traveled to the United States by sea, his traveling companion was one Dr. Lucas, an American who was president of a college in Lahore, Pakistan. Lucas provided Bonhoeffer with expert advice on India. He also invited Bonhoeffer to visit him in Lahore. Bonhoeffer planned to join Lucas on his Indian tour, which was also to include visits to Benares, Allabad, Agra, and Delhi.

   Paul Lehmann, Bonhoeffer's schoolmate and close friend at Union Theological Seminary, took him around the docks in New York. Lehmann knew a freighter captain who would take someone cheaply to India. Klaus, Dietrich's brother, had a sister-in-law in Manila who gave him names of persons to visit at Asian ports. But after further inquiries, Bonhoeffer found that the trip by way of the Pacific would be too expensive. He then focused his attention on America for the time being. This visit to the United States was during the 1930–1931 academic year.

10. 1bid., 406.
11. Ibid.
12. 1bid., 407.
13. Ibid.
14. Ibid.
15. Ibid.
16. Ibid., 408.
17. Ibid., 409.
18. Ibid., 409–15. Now that his option to go to India had been closed, he sought to observe ecumenical experiences among various denominations in Great Britain (e.g., Anglicans, Baptists, Congregationalists, Presbyterians, Methodists, and Quakers). With the Sermon on the Mount in view, Bonhoeffer sought a theological interpretation that would lead to a community in service and spiritual exercises, a witness to social action, a resistance to tyrannical power, and an openness to ecumenism. In his quest he even went to Scotland to converse with his former Union professor John Baillie.

    Bethge, Bonhoeffer's closest friend and biographer, attempts to explain why Bonhoeffer was so intense in his desire to meet and know Gandhi. This is what he says: "In Barcelona, Bonhoeffer had conceived the idea of making a journey to India before going home, at that time his principle thought being to experience true Asian piety. Now he dreamed the dream a second time, but this time his main intention was to study Gandhi's concept of political pacifism at first hand. Again nothing came of it—as indeed to be the case in the third attempt, from London in 1935. But this recurrent dream played an important part in Bonhoeffer's development. His colleagues at home, Barth included, never understood properly his intention. Perhaps only at the end of his life did the nature of this attempt become clear: it was the wish to understand his own tradition of Christianity in light of quite a different way of life and of thinking, and so to find new expression for it" (Eberhard Bethge, *Costly Grace* [New York: Harper & Row, 1979], 42–43).

    Later Bethge writes, "Bonhoeffer considered Gandhi the greatest thinker and activist of nonviolent resistance, which he wanted to study in its original home and form. Perhaps here was an opportunity to discover how a follower of Christ, a Christian pastor, could offer appropriate resistance without repudiating political responsibility" (pp. 75–76).

    See Guy Carter, Rene van Eyden, Hans-Dirk van Hoogstraten, and Jurjen Wiersma, eds., *Bonhoeffer's Ethics: Old Europe and New Frontiers* (Kampen, Netherlands: Kok Pharos Publishing House, 1991). These essays by Bonhoeffer scholars reveal from a European perspective Bonhoeffer's disenchantment with Christianity in the West. There also are essays on his desire to meet Gandhi.
19. Other Howard University religious scholars, such as Benjamin Mays and Howard Thurman, knew Gandhi's life and work in person. William Stuart Nelson, a philosopher of religion and Howard's academic vice president, wrote several learned essays on Gandhi's philosophy. I have presented the Howard University connection with Gandhi in "Gandhi and King: On Conflict Resolution," *Shalom Papers: A Journal of Theology and Public Policy* 2, no. 1 (Spring 2000): 29–42. Erich Geldbach from the University of Bochum, Germany, a colleague of mine during a visiting professorship at Baylor University, has produced a valuable essay titled "Von Gandhi zu Martin Luther King." So far as I know the essay is unpublished.

20. Martin Luther King Jr., *Stride toward Freedom: The Montgomery Story* (San Francisco: Harper & Row, 1958), 96–97. For a detailed description of King's visit to the land of Gandhi in 1959, see Coretta Scott King, *My Life with Martin Luther King, Jr.* (New York: Holt, Rinehart & Winston, 1969), 172–80.

21. Quoted in Robert Ellsberg, ed., *Gandhi on Christianity* (Maryknoll, NY: Orbis Books, 1993), 21–22.

22. Ibid., 22.

23. See John Godsey, *New Studies in Bonhoeffer's Ethics*, Toronto Studies in Theology 30, Bonhoeffer Series 3 (Lewiston, NY: Edwin Mellen Press, 1987), 99. Cf. Gerhard Kittel et al., eds., *Theological Dictionary of the New Testament* (Grand Rapids: Eerdmans, 1964), 1:46.

24. Dietrich Bonhoeffer, *The Cost of Discipleship*, trans. R. H. Fuller (New York: Macmillan, 1959), 176–79.

25. Martin Luther King Jr., *Strength to Love* (Cleveland: Collins-World, 1963), 47–55.

26. Ibid., 51.

27. Ibid., 55.

Chapter 10: The Relationship of Church and State in Bonhoeffer and King

1. John Witte Jr., *Law and Protestantism* (Cambridge: Cambridge University Press, 2002), 3–9. Cf. John Dillenberger, *Martin Luther* (New York: Anchor Books, 1962), chap. 4.

2. William A. Mueller, *Church and State in Luther and Calvin* (Nashville: Broadman Press, 1954), 127–29.

3. John Calvin, *Institutes of the Christian Religion* (Edinburgh: T. & T. Clark, 1895), 4.4:551. Cf. *Calvin's Institutes: Abridged Edition*, ed. Donald K. McKim (Louisville, KY: Westminster John Knox Press, 2001), 124–26. See also W. Stanford Reid, ed., *John Calvin: His Influence in the Western World* (Grand Rapids: Zondervan, 1982).

4. Dietrich Bonhoeffer, *Ethics*, ed. Eberhard Bethge (New York: Macmillan, 1965), 331–32. Bonhoeffer provides a helpful discussion on the state in the history of philosophy and theology prior to the Reformation (see pp. 333–34).

5. Ibid., 336.

6. Ibid., 337–39. Here Bonhoeffer provides a polemic against a natural law version of the state. He insists upon his christological version.

7. Ibid., 340. Bonhoeffer goes on to explain the task of government and its claims against this background (see pp. 341–46).

8. Ibid., 352–53.

9. Ibid., 351–52.

10. Lewis V. Baldwin, "On the Relation of the Christian to the State: The Development of a Kingdom Ethic," in *The Legacy of Martin Luther King, Jr.: The Boundaries of Law, Politics, and Religion*, by Lewis V. Baldwin, with Rufus Burrow Jr. et al. (Notre Dame, IN: University of Notre Dame Press, 2002), 81–85.

11. Ibid., 86.

12. Samuel S. Hill, "Religion and Politics in the South," in *Religion in the South*, ed. Charles R. Wilson (Jackson: University Press of Mississippi, 1985), 144.

13. Baldwin, "On the Relation of the Christian to the State," 99.

14. Quoted in Baldwin, "On the Relation of the Christian to the State," 97–98.

15. Michael G. Long, *Against Us, but for Us: Martin Luther King, Jr., and the State* (Macon, GA: Mercer University Press, 2002), xv. This book is well researched

and thorough in discussing King's views on the state. Cf. Michael Eric Dyson, *I May Not Get There with You: The True Martin Luther King, Jr.* (New York: Free Press, 2000). According to Dyson, King hints at the dialectic (the state as being potentially good or evil) when Dyson observes that due to his religious beliefs, King refused to idolize the state. Despite the charge that he subverted the social order, King was a tireless advocate of democracy (p. 4). See also J. Deotis Roberts, "A Theological Conception of the State," *Journal of Church and State*, May 4, 1962, 66–75.

Though some Baptists want to claim a definite beginning in the New Testament, they really belong to seventeenth-century English Separatism with roots in the Protestant Reformation. In this study I have taken that view. Cf. H. Leon McBeth, *Baptist Heritage* (Nashville: Broadman Press, 1987), 61–62.

Chapter 11: The Context of Decision: Bonhoeffer

1. Elizabeth Raum, *Dietrich Bonhoeffer: Called by God* (New York: Continuum, 2002), 49–53.
2. Ibid., 54–57.
3. Ibid., 57. Cf. Jackson J. Spielvogel, *Hitler and Nazi Germany: A History*, 4th ed. (Upper Saddle River, NJ: Prentice Hall, 2001), 132.
4. Raum, *Dietrich Bonhoeffer*, 58.
5. Dietrich Bonhoeffer, *No Rusty Swords*, ed. Edwin H. Robertson (New York: Harper & Row, 1965), 217.
6. Ibid., 220.
7. Ibid., 220–21.
8. Ibid., 222.
9. John Godsey, *The Theology of Dietrich Bonhoeffer* (Philadelphia: Westminster Press, 1960), 111–12.
10. Ibid., 116–17.
11. Ibid., 118.
12. Martin Walton, ed., *Marginal Communities: The Ethical Enterprise of the Followers of Jesus* (Kampen, Netherlands: Kok Pharos Publishing House, 1994), 7–10.
13. Ibid., 10.
14. Ibid., 11–12.
15. Ibid., 12–13.
16. Ibid., 14–15.
17. Ibid.
18. Ibid., 17–18. Cf. Renate Wind, *Dietrich Bonhoeffer: A Spoke in the Wheel*, trans. John Bowden (Grand Rapids: Eerdmans, 1992), 65–88. For a thorough discussion on Bonhoeffer's understanding of the Old Testament, see Martin Kuske, *The Old Testament as the Book of Christ*, trans. S. T. Kimbrough Jr. (Philadelphia: Westminster Press, 1976).
19. See Franklin H. Littell and Hubert G. Locke, eds., *The German Church Struggle and the Holocaust* (Detroit: Wayne State University Press, 1974), for a series of noble essays on this vital subject. Cf. Detlev J. K. Peukert, *Inside Nazi Germany: Conformity, Opposition, and Racism in Everyday Life*, trans. R. Deveson (New Haven, CT: Yale University Press, 1987). Peukert notes (p. 41) that for Hitler, "anti-Semitism, anti-Bolshevism and anti-capitalism were interchangeable." See J. S. Conway, *The Nazi Persecution of the Churches, 1933–45* (London: Weidenfeld & Nicolson, 1997), chaps. 2 and 3. To get a good look at the theological reinterpretation of the gospel, see Robert P. Ericksen and Susannah

Heschel, eds., *Betrayal: German Churches and the Holocaust* (Minneapolis: Fortress Press, 1999), chaps. 2 and 6.

Chapter 12: The Context of Decision: King

1. Benjamin Quarles, *The Negro in the Making of America*, 3rd ed. (New York: Simon & Schuster, 1996), 275–76.
2. Ibid., 276–77.
3. Ibid.
4. Ibid., 279–80. Quarles provides a good look at how the *Brown* decision influenced blacks and whites in many areas, such as the arts and sports (pp. 277–91).
5. See my essay, "Christian Conscience and Legal Discrimination," *Journal of Religious Thought* 19, no. 2 (1962): 157–61.
6. Quarles, *Negro in the Making of America*, 291–95. Many organizations now entered the field to bring about progress in race relations. Among these were King's Southern Christian Leadership Conference (SCLC), the Congress on Racial Equality (CORE), the Student Nonviolent Coordinating Committee (SNCC), the Northern Student Movement (NSM), and others.
7. See Clayborne Carson, ed., *The Autobiography of Martin Luther King, Jr.* (New York: Warner Books, 1998), chaps. 17–19.
8. Ibid., 17–18.
9. Ibid., 218.
10. Ibid., 222–23.
11. Ibid., 228. In an NBC evening news report on August 30, 2003, it was reported that in 1967, King referred to the racial situation as "a nightmare."
12. William D. Watley, *Roots of Resistance: The Nonviolent Ethic of Martin Luther King, Jr.* (Valley Forge, PA: Judson Press, 1985), 63–70. Cf. David J. Garrow, *Bearing the Cross: Martin Luther King, Jr., and the Southern Christian Leadership Conference* (New York: William Morrow & Co., 1986), 173–230.
13. Watley, *Roots of Resistance*, 70–73.
14. Ibid., 74–95.
15. Ibid., 88. Cf. Garrow, *Bearing the Cross*, chap. 7.
16. Watley, *Roots of Resistance*, 88–90.

Chapter 13: Speaking Truth to Power: Bonhoeffer

1. Larry Rasmussen, with Renate Bethge, *Dietrich Bonhoeffer: His Significance for North Americans* (Minneapolis: Fortress Press, 1990), chap. 7.
2. See Charles Kimball, *When Religion Becomes Evil* (San Francisco: HarperSanFrancisco, 2002). This is a valuable resource for understanding the evil potential of religions. Cf. Jerome Walters, *One Aryan Nation under God* (Cleveland: Pilgrim Press, 2000). This volume is a stark reminder of the religious motivation behind racism inspired by the ghost of Hitler in our own country.
3. See James Burtness, *Shaping the Future: The Ethics of Dietrich Bonhoeffer* (Philadelphia: Fortress Press, 1985), chap. 1. Burtness treats in this work the centrality of Jesus Christ, the relationship of the doctrine of the church to ethics, the rejection of two-sphere thinking, rationality and responsibility, and the place of time and history in ethics.
4. Ibid., 28–29.
5. Benjamin Reist, *The Promise of Bonhoeffer* (Philadelphia: J. B. Lippincott, 1969), 118–20.
6. Dietrich Bonhoeffer, *Ethics*, trans. N. H. Smith (New York: Macmillan, 1978), 128–29.

7. Rasmussen, *Dietrich Bonhoeffer*, 89–91.
8. Dietrich Bonhoeffer, *Act and Being*, trans. Bernard Noble (New York: Harper & Row, 1962), 90–91.
9. Rasmussen, *Dietrich Bonhoeffer*, 95.
10. Dietrich Bonhoeffer, *No Rusty Swords*, ed. Edwin H. Robertson, trans. J. Bowden and E. Bethge (London: Collins, 1970), 46–47.
11. Rasmussen, *Dietrich Bonhoeffer*, 98.
12. Bonhoeffer, *Ethics*, 281.
13. Ibid., 279–280.
14. Rasmussen, *Dietrich Bonhoeffer*, 108–9.
15. Ibid., 110.
16. Keith Clements, "Ecumenical Witness for Peace," in *The Cambridge Companion to Dietrich Bonhoeffer*, ed. John W. de Gruchy (Cambridge: Cambridge University Press, 1999), 154–63.
17. Quoted in Clements, "Ecumenical Witness for Peace," 162. Cf. Bonhoeffer, *No Rusty Swords*, 291.
18. Rasmussen, *Dietrich Bonhoeffer*, 47.
19. Bonhoeffer, *Ethics*, 350–51.
20. Rasmussen, *Dietrich Bonhoeffer*, 47–48.
21. Eberhard Bethge, *Costly Grace* (New York: Harper & Row, 1979), 92–94. Bethge also provides a careful account of events that led Bonhoeffer to make his decision to join the conspiracy (pp. 95–98).
22. Dietrich Bonhoeffer, *The Way to Freedom*, ed. Edwin H. Robertson, trans. Edwin H. Robertson and John Bowden (New York: Harper & Row, 1966), 2:246.
23. Ibid.
24. John de Gruchy, *Dietrich Bonhoeffer: Witness to Jesus Christ* (Minneapolis: Fortress Press, 1991), 30.
25. Quoted in Bethge, *Costly Grace*, 110. Cf. Bonhoeffer, *Letters and Papers from Prison* (London: SCM Press, 1971), 174.
26. G. K. A. Bell, foreword to *The Cost of Discipleship*, rev. ed., by Dietrich Bonhoeffer (New York: Macmillan, 1959), 7.
27. Ibid., 8.
28. G. Leibholz, "Memoir," in Bonhoeffer, *Cost of Discipleship*, 14.
29. Ibid., 29–32.
30. Bell, foreword to *Cost of Discipleship*, 7.
31. See Clifford Green, "Bonhoeffer: No! To Paul Hill," *International Bonhoeffer Society Newsletter* no. 83 (Fall 2003): 10.
32. Dietrich Bonhoeffer, "True Patriotism," in "Letters, Lectures, and Notes, 1939–1945," from *Collected Works*, ed. E. H. Robertson, trans. E. H. Robertson and John Bowden (New York: Harper & Row, 1973), 3:245. One is reminded of the martyrdom of Socrates, who observed, as he drank the poisonous hemlock, that his death was the beginning of life. While Socrates based his statement on belief in the immortality of the soul, Bonhoeffer no doubt put his trust in the Christian doctrine of the resurrection.

Chapter 14: Speaking Truth to Power: King

1. The Boston personalists seem to want to claim final credit for the direction in which King's witness was played out. Although they made a powerful impression upon him, there were many other influences that helped to shape his thoughts, life, and actions. For the claims of the Boston personalists, see Walter G.

Muelder, "Philosophical and Theological Influences in the Thought and Action of Martin Luther King, Jr.," in David J. Garrow, ed., *Martin Luther King, Jr. and the Civil Rights Movement* (Brooklyn, NY: Carlson Publishing, Inc., 1989), 3:691–701. Cf. L. Harold DeWolf, "Martin Luther King, Jr. as Theologian," in the same volume. See also Paul Deats and Carol Robb, eds., *The Boston Personalist Tradition in Philosophy, Social Ethics, and Theology* (Macon, GA: Mercer University Press, 1986), 4–5.

2. King arrived at Crozer on the eve of his adulthood, having been shaped by the black experience of racist oppression. He had made the decision to become a minister as well as to seek the freedom of his people before he arrived in Chester, Pennsylvania. His parents made sure that he would be anchored in the black family, community, and church in Chester and later in Boston. Thus, while King engaged in advanced study, he never lost contact with this orientation in the black heritage. I can affirm the importance of this arrangement from my experience at Hartford Seminary and my anchor in the Union Baptist Church there. Cf. Lewis V. Baldwin, *There Is a Balm in Gilead: The Cultural Roots of Martin Luther King, Jr.* (Minneapolis: Fortress Press, 1991).

3. See Martin Luther King Jr., *Strength to Love* (New York: Harper & Row, 1963), 58. Cf. J. Deotis Roberts, *Black Theology in Dialogue* (Philadelphia: Westminster Press, 1987), chap. 9.

4. King, *Strength to Love*, 60.

5. See John J. Ansbro, *Martin Luther King, Jr.: The Making of a Mind* (Maryknoll, NY: Orbis Books, 1982), 160. Ansbro's study not only discusses King's thought but it places his ideas in historical context as well.

6. See Carl H. Marbury, "An Excursus on the Biblical and Theological Rhetoric of Martin Luther King, Jr.," in *Essays in Honor of Martin Luther King, Jr.*, ed. John H. Cartwright (Evanston, IL: Leiffer Social and Religious Research, 1971), 14–20.

7. Malcolm X came to Selma during the protest for voting rights and indicated that he was present to reinforce a decision. He was not present to oppose King's effort. Cf. Lawrence E. Carter Jr., *Walking Integrity: Benjamin E. Mays, Mentor to Martin Luther King, Jr.* (Macon, GA: Mercer University Press, 1998), chap. 8.

8. Kenneth L. Smith and Ira G. Zepp, Jr., *Search for the Beloved Community: The Thinking of Martin Luther King, Jr.* (Valley Forge, PA: Judson Press, 1998), chap. 1.

9. King applied to Yale University but was not admitted. He was admitted to the University of Edinburgh, where I received my PhD. For some reason, King decided to study at Boston University. Perhaps he was already impressed with personalism. This, in my judgment, was an important choice, since Edinburgh at the time (mid-1950s) was not a suitable place to study theological ethics. It was a profound center for classical studies, but the kind of mission that King was about did not move the faculty there. Personalism was a system of thought that could be put more readily into the cause of social justice.

10. Rufus Burrow Jr., "Personalism, the Objective Moral Order, and Moral Law in the Work of Martin Luther King, Jr.," in *The Legacy of Martin Luther King, Jr.: The Boundaries of Law, Politics, and Religion*, by Lewis V. Baldwin et al. (Notre Dame, IN: University of Notre Dame Press, 2002), 227–28.

11. Burrow, "Personalism, the Objective Moral Order, and Moral Law," 222–23.

12. Ibid., 224.

13. Ibid., 225. Cf. J. Deotis Roberts, *Liberation and Reconciliation: A Black Theology* (Philadelphia: Westminster Press, 1971), chap. 4.
14. Ansbro, *Martin Luther King, Jr.*, 110–25.
15. Martin Luther King Jr., *Stride toward Freedom: The Montgomery Story* (New York: Harper & Row, 1958), 44.
16. Quoted in Ansbro, *Martin Luther King, Jr.*, 126.
17. Ansbro, *Martin Luther King, Jr.*, 132–34. This author provides a detailed account of Gandhi's project that is invaluable.
18. Ibid., 134.
19. William D. Watley, *Roots of Resistance: The Nonviolent Ethic of Martin Luther King, Jr.* (Valley Forge, PA: Judson Press, 1985), chap. 5. Watley has captured well the essence of King's nonviolent ethic. Even his critique is useful.
20. King, *Strength to Love*, 46.
21. At this point we need to be reminded of King's engagement with the systemic evil of racism in the United States. Several sources by African American religious thinkers should be examined. I will list a few:

    1. Vincent Harding, *Martin Luther King: The Inconvenient Hero* (Maryknoll, NY: Orbis Books, 1996), chap. 3.
    2. Watley, *Roots of Resistance*, chap. 5.
    3. Baldwin, *Legacy of Martin Luther King, Jr.* See esp. the second and third essays, by Baldwin, in which the author discusses King's views and encounters with political realities in the United States. The essay by Barbara A. Holmes and Susan H. Winfield titled "King, the Constitution and the Courts" is also very valuable.
    4. Michael Eric Dyson, *I May Not Get There with You: The True Martin Luther King, Jr.* (New York: Free Press, 2000), 1–50. The entire book is factual, candid, and critical.
    5. Clayborne Carson, ed. *The Autobiography of Martin Luther King, Jr.* (New York: Warner Books, 1998). The value of this book is that it presents King's own interpretation of events in his life.

22. Carson, ed., *Autobiography of Martin Luther King, Jr.*, 231.
23. Ibid., 237.
24. Ibid., chap. 21.
25. Ibid., chap. 22. It is tempting here to provide a blow-by-blow account of King's insistent attack upon racism through the 1960s, but this book is about how his faith and thought informed his action. Besides, many excellent works recount this history. I recommend the companion volumes by Taylor Branch: *Parting the Waters: America in the King Years, 1954–1963* (New York: Simon & Schuster, 1988); and *Pillar of Fire: America in the King Years, 1963–1965* (New York: Simon & Schuster, 1998).
26. I was in Chicago during the summer of 1965. My purpose there was to do research at the University of Chicago. Advanced African American students wanted to know why I was not in the civil rights demonstrations. They also asked me what I thought they should do. Some felt that they should give up their studies and devote themselves full time to King's movement. The struggle for freedom, I explained, would be continuous, and we would need persons intellectually qualified to be leaders. They seemed encouraged to continue their studies.
    While in Chicago, I connected with the black pastors in their meetings. Some pastors were not interested in social justice issues. Those who were supported

King firmly. However, one nationally known pastor, Joseph Jackson, strongly opposed King's approach to black freedom. Jackson, pastor of the Olivet Baptist Church and president of the National Baptist Convention, Inc., was a powerful advocate of a gradual approach to better racial relations. The differences between King and Jackson led to a division in black Baptist circles and the founding of a new convention in 1961, the Progressive Baptist Convention. See Albert A. Avant Jr., *The Social Teachings of the Progressive National Baptist Convention, Inc., since 1961: A Critical Analysis of the Least, the Lost, and the Left-out* (New York: Routledge, 2004), chap. 2. King was put out of the National Baptist Convention, Inc., for ideological reasons.

27. Stanley Levison was one Jewish supporter. See Branch, *Parting the Waters*, 243, 381. Rabbi Abraham J. Heschel was another ardent Jewish supporter of King's movement. See Harding, *Martin Luther King*, 82–86.

28. Carson, ed., *Autobiography of Martin Luther King, Jr.*, 311.

29. Ernest Shaw Lyght, *The Religious and Philosophical Foundations in the Thought of Martin Luther King, Jr.* (New York: Vantage Press, 1972), 78–79. Cf. Elijah Muhammad, *Message to the Black Man in America* (Chicago: Mosque no. 2, 1965), 163–64. See also Kenneth B. Clark, *Dark Ghetto* (New York: Harper & Row, 1965), 214–19; and C. Eric Lincoln, *The Black Muslims in America* (Boston: Beacon Press, 1961), 152.

30. Lyght, *Religious and Philosophical Foundations*, 80.

31. Here the thought of Brightman on evil and God came into play. Brightman had asserted that power is neutral as a value. It can achieve good as well as evil ends. King, however, did not accept Brightman's decision that God is limited in power.

32. Lyght, *Religious and Philosophical Foundations*, 84–85. On King's interpretation of "black power," see Carson, ed., *Autobiography of Martin Luther King, Jr.*, chap. 29. Cf. Ansbro, *Martin Luther King, Jr.*, 211–30.

33. By this time, King had arrived at his conception of what he called "a world-house," in which all humans must learn to live in friendship. He concluded that not only Christianity but also all the major religions of the world sought the reign of love among humans.

34. Lyght, *Religious and Philosophical Foundations*, 85.

35. Carson, ed., *Autobiography of Martin Luther King, Jr.*, 350–51.

36. Ibid., 351.

37. Ibid.

38. Ibid., 354–55.

39. Ibid., 358–59. Upon his return from India King told his wife that to be dedicated to a cause, in the spirit of Gandhi, one would have to give up all. He said to Coretta, "You know a man who dedicates himself to a cause doesn't need a family." See Coretta S. King, *My Life with Martin Luther King, Jr.* (New York: Holt, Rinehart & Winston, 1969), 178. Of course, she was able to put a positive interpretation on this statement. She believed he was dealing with the conflict between love and duty. She felt he needed her and the children to continue the struggle for black freedom.

40. Carson, ed., *Autobiography of Martin Luther King, Jr.*, 105, 197.

41. Frederick L. Downing, *To See the Promised Land* (Macon, GA: Mercer University Press, 1987), 280.

42. C. King, *My Life with Martin*, 318–19.

43. Even if Coretta was able to accept King's death as a reality, it was a terrible blow to their four children. Two of them have revealed in print how their father's life

and death impressed them. King's youngest daughter, Bernice, is a minister with both law and theology degrees. She has lectured and preached to thousands. See Bernice A. King, *Hard Questions, Heart Answers* (New York: Broadway Books, 1996). Dexter, the youngest son, has struggled to come to terms with his father's death for a lifetime. See Dexter Scott King, *Growing Up King* (New York: Warner Books, 2003). The initial reaction to King's death among the children is described in C. King, *My Life with Martin*, 321–23.
44. C. King, *My Life with Martin*, 104–5.
45. Carson, ed., *Autobiography of Martin Luther King, Jr.*, 365–66.
46. Ibid., 265.

Conclusion

1. J. Deotis Roberts, *From Puritanism to Platonism in Seventeenth Century England* (The Hague, Netherlands: Martinus Nijhoff, 1968).
2. Thurman let me know in a personal dialogue that his concern was "Jesus." He had no use for christological dogmas. As a theologian, I have a concern for both the humanity and divinity of Jesus Christ. In my view, human sin makes atonement on the cross necessary. A human moral example can point to the right path, but it has no power to redeem us from sin. Thus, the balance of a viable Christology should affirm that the Jesus of history is the Christ of faith. Furthermore, a well-proportioned Christology should be grounded in the doctrine of the Trinity as well.
3. Quoted by David J. Garrow, *Bearing the Cross* (New York: William Morrow & Co., 1986), epigraph page. King appears to accept the "God-consciousness" in Schleiermacher as an element in his Christology. This is anti-Barthian and would not appeal to Bonhoeffer.
4. Dietrich Bonhoeffer, *The Cost of Discipleship*, rev. ed. (New York: Macmillan, 1959), chap. 1.
5. George D. Kelsey, *Racism and the Christian Understanding of Man* (New York: Charles Scribner's Sons, 1965), 9.
6. See John A. Phillips, *Christ for Us in the Theology of Dietrich Bonhoeffer* (New York: Harper, 1964).
7. Some of the best reflection on the Sermon on the Mount I am aware of is by Professor Glen H. Stassen of Fuller Theological Seminary. Glen's thought on this subject is acclaimed by ethicists, biblical scholars, and systematic theologians. Many insights in this volume have been inspired by personal conversations with him and by reading his written work on the Sermon on the Mount. See his essay "Bonhoeffer's Use of the Sermon on the Mount and the Pluralistic Context of the Conspiracy," *Journal of the Society of Biblical Literature* 122, no. 2 (2003): 267–308.

Select Bibliography

Works by Dietrich Bonhoeffer

Books

The Cost of Discipleship. Rev. ed. New York: Macmillan, 1959.

Ethics. Edited by Eberhard Bethge. New York: Touchstone, 1995.

True Patriotism. In *Collected Works*, vol. 3, edited by E. H. Robertson, translated by E. H. Robertson and John Bowden. New York: Harper & Row, 1973.

Works. Minneapolis: Fortress Press, 1986–2003.

    Volume 1: *Sanctorum Communio: A Theological Study of the Sociology of the Church*. Edited by Clifford Green. Translated by Reinhard Krauss and Nancy Lukens. 1986.

    Volume 2: *Act and Being: Transcendental Philosophy and Ontology in Systematic Theology*. Edited by Wayne Whitson Floyd Jr. Translated by H. Martin Rumscheidt. 1996.

    Volume 3: *Creation and Fall: A Theological Exposition of Genesis 1–3*. Edited by John W. De Gruchy. Translated by Douglas Stephens. 1977.

    Volume 4: *Discipleship*. Edited by Geffrey B. Kelly and John D. Godsey. Translated by Barbara Green and Reinhard Krauss. 2001.

    Volume 5: *Life Together/Prayerbook of the Bible*. Edited by Geffrey B. Kelly. Translated by Daniel W. Bloesch and James H. Buttress. 1996.

    Volume 7: *Fiction from Tegel Prison*. Edited by Clifford J. Green. Translated by Nancy Lukens. 2000.

    Volume 9: *The Young Bonhoeffer, 1918–1927*. Edited by Paul Duane Matheny, Clifford J. Green, and Marshall D. Johnson. Translated by Mary C. Nebelsick and Douglas W. Scott. 2003.

Collections of Papers

Kelly, Geffrey B. and F. Burton Nelson, eds. *Testament to Freedom: The Essential Writings of Dietrich Bonhoeffer*. Rev. ed. San Francisco: HarperSanFrancisco, 1995.

"The Paul L. Lehmann Papers" (correspondence with D. Bonhoeffer), nos. 2:38; 6:36; 15:85; 20:27; 27:6; 35:1; 45:6; 59:6; 60:14. In Princeton Theological Seminary Archives, 1999.

Works about Dietrich Bonhoeffer

Books

Bosanquet, Mary. *The Life and Death of Dietrich Bonhoeffer*. New York: Harper & Row, 1968.

Bethge, Eberhard. *Costly Grace*. New York: Harper & Row, 1979.

———. *Dietrich Bonhoeffer: A Biography*. Rev. ed. Philadelphia: Fortress Press, 2000.

Bethge, Eberhard, Renate Bethge, and Christian Gremmels, eds. *Dietrich Bonhoeffer: A Life in Pictures.* Philadelphia: Fortress Press, 1986.

Day, Thomas I. *Dietrich Bonhoeffer on Christian Community and Common Sense.* Toronto Studies in Theology 11. New York: Edwin Mellen Press, 1982.

De Gruchy, John W. *Bonhoeffer for a New Day: Theology in a Time of Transition.* Grand Rapids: Eerdmans, 1997.

———, ed. *The Cambridge Companion to Dietrich Bonhoeffer.* Cambridge: Cambridge University Press, 1999.

Feil, Ernst. *The Theology of Dietrich Bonhoeffer.* Philadelphia: Fortress Press, 1985.

Godsey, John D., and Geffrey B. Kelley, eds. *Ethical Responsibility: Bonhoeffer's Legacy to the Churches.* New York: Edwin Mellen Press, 1981.

Green, Clifford. *Bonhoeffer: A Theology of Sociality.* Rev. ed. Grand Rapids: Eerdmans, 1994.

Hopper, David A. *A Dissent on Bonhoeffer.* Philadelphia: Fortress Press, 1957.

Kelley, Geffrey B. *Liberating Faith: Bonhoeffer's Message for Today.* Minneapolis: Augsburg, 1984.

Klassen, A. J., ed. *A Bonhoeffer Legacy.* Grand Rapids: Eerdmans, 1981.

Leibholz-Bonhoeffer, Sabine. *The Bonhoeffers: A Portrait of a Family.* Chicago: Covenant Publications, 1994.

Pangritz, Anders. *Karl Barth in the Theology of Dietrich Bonhoeffer.* Grand Rapids: Eerdmans, 2000.

Peck, William J., ed. *New Studies in Bonhoeffer's Ethics.* Lewiston, NY: Edwin Mellen Press, 1987.

Phillips, John A. *Christ for Us in the Theology of Dietrich Bonhoeffer.* New York: Harper & Row, 1967.

Rasmussen, Larry, with Renate Bethge. *Dietrich Bonhoeffer: His Significance for North Americans.* Minneapolis: Fortress Press, 1990.

Raum, Elizabeth. *Dietrich Bonhoeffer: Called by God.* New York: Continuum, 2002.

Smith, Ronald Gregor. *World Come of Age.* London: Collins, 1967.

Bibliographies of Bonhoeffer Works

Feil, Ernst. *Bonhoeffer Studies in Germany: A Survey of Recent Literature.* Philadelphia: International Bonhoeffer Society, 1997.

Floyd, Wayne, and Clifford Green, eds. *A Bonhoeffer Bibliography.* Evanston, IL: American Theological Library Association, 1992.

Works by Martin Luther King Jr.

Books

The Measure of a Man. Boston: Pilgrim Press, 1968.

The Papers of Martin Luther King, Jr. 4 vols. Edited by Clayborne Carson et al. Berkeley: University of California Press, 1992–1997.

Strength to Love. New York: Harper & Row, 1963.

Stride toward Freedom: The Montgomery Story. San Francisco: Harper & Row, 1958.

The Trumpet of Conscience. San Francisco: Harper & Row, 1968.

Where Do We Go from Here? Boston: Beacon Press, 1967.

Dissertation

A Comparison of the Conception of God in the Thinking of Paul Tillich and Henry Nelson Wieman. Ann Arbor, MI: University Microfilms, 1968.

Collection of Writings

Washington, James Melvin, ed. *A Testament of Hope: The Essential Writings and Speeches of Martin Luther King, Jr.* San Francisco: Harper & Row, 1986.

Books about Martin Luther King Jr.

Abernathy, Ralph D. *And the Walls Came Tumbling Down.* New York: Harper & Row, 1989.

Ansbro, John T. *Martin Luther King, Jr.: The Making of a Mind.* Maryknoll, NY: Orbis Books, 1982.

Baldwin, Lewis V. *To Make the Wounded Whole: The Cultural Legacy of Martin Luther King, Jr.* Minneapolis: Fortress Press, 1990.

Branch, Taylor. *Parting the Waters: America in the King Years, 1954–1963.* New York: Simon & Schuster, 1988.

———. *Pillar of Fire: America in the King Years, 1963–1965.* New York: Simon & Schuster, 1998.

Cone, James H. *Martin and Malcolm and America: A Dream or a Nightmare?* Maryknoll, NY: Orbis Books, 1992.

Dyson, Eric. *I May Not Get There with You: The True Martin Luther King, Jr.* New York: Touchstone, 2001.

Erskine, Noel L. *King among the Theologians.* Cleveland: Pilgrim Press, 1994.

Garrow, David J., ed. *Martin Luther King, Jr. and the Civil Rights Movement.* Brooklyn, NY: William Morrow & Co., 1986.

King, Coretta Scott. *My Life with Martin Luther King, Jr.* New York: Holt, Rinehart & Winston, 1969.

Lewis, David L. *King: A Biography.* 2nd ed. Urbana: University of Illinois Press, 1978.

Long, Michael G. *Against Us, but for Us: Martin Luther King, Jr., and the State.* Macon, GA: Mercer University Press, 2002.

Lyght, Ernest S. *The Religious and Philosophical Foundations in the Thought of Martin Luther King, Jr.* New York: Vantage Press, 1972.

Smith, Kenneth L., and Ira G. Zepp Jr. *Search for the Beloved Community: The Thinking of Martin Luther King, Jr.* Valley Forge, PA: Judson Press, 1974.

Watley, William D. *Roots of Resistance: The Nonviolent Ethic of Martin Luther King, Jr.* Valley Forge, PA: Judson Press, 1985.

General Bibliography

Baranowski, Shelley. *The Confessing Church, Conservative Elites, and the Nazi State.* Lewiston, NY: Edwin Mellen Press, 1986.

Battle, Michael. *Reconciliation: The Ubuntu Theology of Desmond Tutu.* Cleveland: Pilgrim Press, 1997.

Baum, Gregory, and Harold Wells, eds. *The Reconciliation of Peoples: Challenge to the Churches.* Geneva, Switzerland: WCC Publications, 1997.

Bowne, Borden P. *Theism.* New York: American Book Co., 1902.

Brown, Charles C. *A Reinhold Niebuhr Reader.* Philadelphia: Trinity Press International, 1992.

Chatterjee, Margaret. *Gandhi's Religious Thought.* Notre Dame, IN: University of Notre Dame Press, 1983.

Conway, John S. *The Nazi Persecution of the Churches, 1933–1945.* London: Weidenfeld & Nelson, 1968.

Deats, Paul, and Carol Robb., eds. *The Boston Personalist Tradition in Philosophy, Social Ethics, and Theology*. Macon, GA: Mercer University Press, 1986.

De Gruchy, John W. *Reconciliation: Restoring Justice*. Minneapolis: Fortress Press, 2002.

DeWolf, L. Harold. *A Theology of the Living Church*. New York: Harper & Brothers, 1953.

Duff, Nancy J. *Humanization and the Politics of God: The Koinonia Ethics of Paul Lehmann*. Grand Rapids: Eerdmans, 1992.

Ericksen, Robert P., and Susannah Heschel, eds. *Betrayal: German Churches and the Holocaust*. Minneapolis: Fortress Press, 1999.

Farmer, H. H. *Reconciliation and Religion: Some Aspects of the Uniqueness of Christianity as a Reconciling Faith*. Edited by C. H. Partridge. Lewiston, NY: Edwin Mellen Press, 1998.

Feige, Franz G. M. *The Varieties of Protestantism in Nazi Germany*. Lewiston, NY: Edwin Mellen Press, 1990.

Gushee, David P. *The Righteous Gentiles of the Holocaust*. Minneapolis: Fortress Press, 1995.

Handy, Robert T., ed. *The Social Gospel in America*. New York: Oxford University Press, 1966.

Hull, Mary. *Rosa Parks*. Springfield, PA: Chelsea House Publishing, 1994.

Kelsey, George D. *Racism and the Christian Understanding of Man*. New York: Charles Scribner's Sons, 1965.

Lehmann, Paul. *Ethics in a Christian Context*. New York: Harper & Row, 1963.

———. *The Transfiguration of Politics*. New York: Harper & Row, 1975.

Littell, Franklin H., and Hubert G. Locke, eds. *The German Church Struggle and the Holocaust*. Detroit: Wayne State University Press, 1974.

Matheson, Peter, ed. *The Third Reich and the Christian Churches*. Edinburgh: T. & T. Clark, 1981.

McClendon, James W., Jr. *Biography as Theology: How Life Stories Can Remake Today's Theology*. Philadelphia: Trinity Press International, 1990.

———. *Systematic Theology*. Vol. 1, *Ethics*. Nashville: Abingdon Press, 1986.

Mueller, William A. *Church and State in Luther and Calvin*. Nashville: Broadman Press, 1954.

Niebuhr, Reinhold. *Moral Man and Immoral Society*. New York: Charles Scribner's Sons, 1932.

Osborne, Robert T. *The Barmen Declaration as a Paradigm for a Theology of the American Church*. New York: Edwin Mellen Press, 1991.

Parks, Rosa, with Gregory J. Reed. *Quiet Strength: The Faith, the Hope, and the Heart of a Woman Who Changed a Nation*. Grand Rapids: Zondervan, 1994.

Peukert, Detlev J. K. *Inside Nazi Germany: Conformity, Opposition, and Racism in Everyday Life*. Translated by R. Deveson. New Haven, CT: Yale University Press, 1987.

Quarles, Benjamin. *The Negro in the Making of America*. 3rd ed. New York: Simon & Schuster, 1996.

Reid, W. Stanford, ed. *John Calvin: His Influence in the Western World*. Grand Rapids: Zondervan, 1982.

Roberts, J. Deotis. "Gandhi and King: On Conflict Resolution." *Shalom Papers: A Journal of Theology and Public Policy* 2, no. 2 (Spring 2000): 29–42.

———. *Liberation and Reconciliation: A Black Theology*. Philadelphia: Westminster Press, 1971.

———. "Victory over Violence.' *Shaw Divinity School Journal* 2, no. 1 (Fall 1997): 23–30.

Schlesinger, Arthur M., Jr. *Hitler.* Springfield, PA: Chelsea House Publishers, 1985.

Schreiter, Robert J. *The Ministry of Reconciliation: Spirituality and Strategies.* Maryknoll, NY: Orbis Books, 1998.

Tillich, Paul. *Against the Third Reich: Paul Tillich's Wartime Addresses to Nazi Germany.* Edited by Ronald H. Stone and Matthew Lon Weaver. Louisville, KY: Westminster John Knox Press, 1998.

West, Cornel. *Prophesy Deliverance! An Afro-American Revolutionary Christianity.* Philadelphia: Westminster Press, 1982.

Wilmore, Gayraud S. *Black Religion and Black Radicalism: An Interpretation of the Religious History of African Americans.* 3rd ed. Maryknoll, NY: Orbis Books, 1998.

Wink, Walter. *Violence and Nonviolence in South Africa.* Philadelphia: New Society Publishers, 1987.

Zuck, Lowell H. *Christianity and Revolution: Radical Christian Testimonies, 1520–1650.* Philadelphia: Temple University Press, 1975.

Index